Martha Stewart's Cookie Perfection

Martha Stewart's Cookie Perfection

100+ Recipes to Take Your Sweet Treats to the Next Level

From the Kitchens of Martha Stewart Living

Clarkson Potter/Publishers
New York

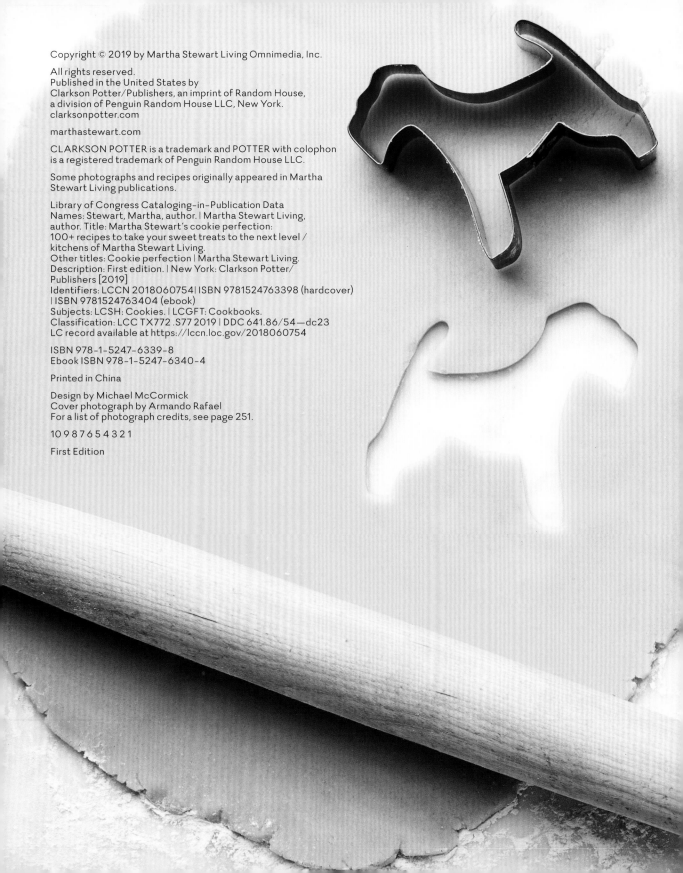

Published in the United States by
Clarkson Potter/Publishers, an imprint of Random House,
a division of Penguin Random House LLC, New York.
clarksonpotter.com

marthastewart.com

CLARKSON POTTER is a trademark and POTTER with colophon
is a registered trademark of Penguin Random House LLC.

Some photographs and recipes originally appeared in Martha
Stewart Living publications.

Library of Congress Cataloging-in-Publication Data
Names: Stewart, Martha, author. | Martha Stewart Living,
author. Title: Martha Stewart's cookie perfection:
100+ recipes to take your sweet treats to the next level /
kitchens of Martha Stewart Living.
Other titles: Cookie perfection | Martha Stewart Living.
Description: First edition. | New York: Clarkson Potter/
Publishers [2019]
Identifiers: LCCN 2018060754| ISBN 9781524763398 (hardcover)
| ISBN 9781524763404 (ebook)
Subjects: LCSH: Cookies. | LCGFT: Cookbooks.
Classification: LCC TX772 .S77 2019 | DDC 641.86/54—dc23
LC record available at https://lccn.loc.gov/2018060754

ISBN 978-1-5247-6339-8
Ebook ISBN 978-1-5247-6340-4

Printed in China

Design by Michael McCormick
Cover photograph by Armando Rafael
For a list of photograph credits, see page 251.

10 9 8 7 6 5 4 3 2 1

First Edition

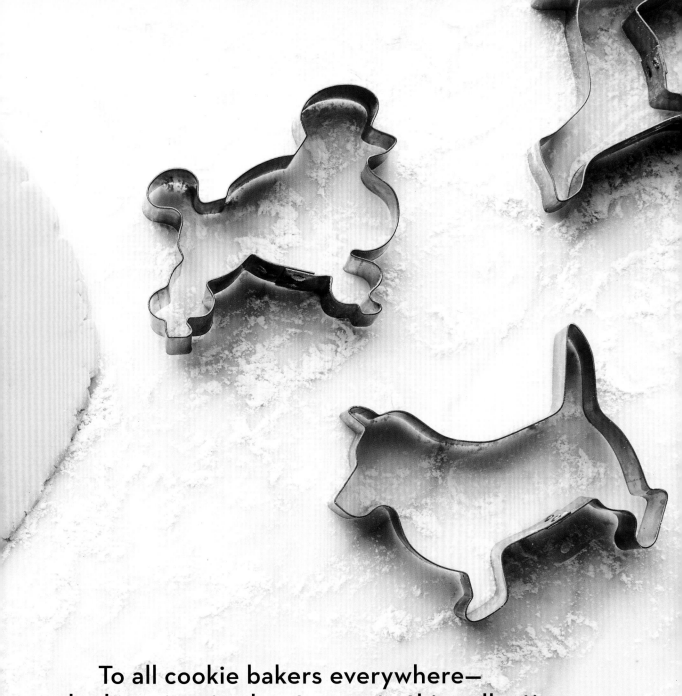

To all cookie bakers everywhere—
who have inspired us to create this collection
of delectable sweets

4
Giant Cookies

5
Tools of the Trade

6
Cookies by Any Other Name

7
Celebration Cookies

8
The Basics

Have a Cookie

When you look through the pages of this book (our ninety-fifth, by the way), you will agree that the general definition of a cookie—"a small flat or slightly raised cake"—is inadequate and even misleading, given the fact that America's favorite dessert has assumed so many incarnations, so many sizes and shapes and flavors.

With this book, we are helping to redefine what cookies can be. No longer are they all small, flat, and sweet. Some are made from pastry doughs like phyllo, pâte brisée, or pâte sucrée. Many are large with an abundance of ingredients, like the Kitchen-Sink Cookie in the "Giant Cookies" chapter, but a few have only four or five ingredients, like the meringues. Others are shaped into crescents, squares, or diamonds and then layered, filled, frosted, dipped, or sugared. Most are baked once, but a couple are baked twice. A number of them can even be described as "sandwiches," such as the lime cookies and the peanut-butter ones you'll find in the "Some Assembly Required" chapter.

It is our belief that this book will open up for you, the home baker, a new realm of cookie perfection. We hope that once you bake one—pick your favorite or start with one of mine, Molasses-Ginger Crisps—you will bake many more, and that you will experiment with flavors and ingredients, trying every recipe in this book. We would love for you to share your experiences, so be sure to post photos of your cookies on social media—it will be fun for all of us to see how you've used this book and enjoyed these recipes.

Happy baking!

Martha Stewart

Golden Rules

1. Take it to the next level.

The recipes in this book make ordinary cookies absolutely extraordinary. Whether classics with a twist, like the Tahini Cookies (page 58) and the Key Lime Sablés (page 73), or a dressed-up creation such as the Flower-Embellished Wreaths (page 24), these treats will introduce you to new flavors, textures, and techniques. We utilized equipment that isn't traditionally used for cookies (think madeleine pans and meat mallets), tried new toppings, and tested unusual flavor combinations for old favorites. But above all, we made sure every cookie was delicious.

2. Be prepared.

To avoid any surprises, read through the recipe before getting started, and have your ingredients measured and prepped. Does the butter need to be at room temperature or melted? Should the nuts be toasted and the chocolate chopped? Have you measured the dry ingredients? A good *mise en place* ensures a smooth baking process.

3. Get to know your oven.

All ovens are different and may vary in temperature, so it's smart to keep a stand-alone thermometer in the oven for accuracy. Since most cookies are small and don't bake for very long, you should set a timer and also keep an eye out for other doneness cues. Some cookies should be dry and firm to the touch, others golden at the edges or just barely set.

4. Find the sweet spot.

For one sheet of cookies, place the rack in the center of the oven, in the middle position. If baking two sheets at a time, racks should be in the upper and lower thirds. Halfway through the baking time, rotate the sheets top to bottom and turn them front to back to ensure even baking.

5. Line the baking sheets.

Line baking sheets with parchment or silicone baking mats for easy cleanup and even baking. They provide some insulation and can prevent scorching on the bottom of your cookies.

6. Take time to chill.

If a recipe calls for chilling the cookie dough, don't skip this important step. (Be sure to factor chilling and resting into your total baking time.) Chilling keeps butter solid, so the dough is less likely to spread during baking. It also concentrates flavor, allowing the sugar time to absorb more liquid, resulting in golden-colored cookies with chewy, crispy spots throughout.

7. Store cookies properly.

Let cookies cool completely before storing, as trapped heat will make them soggy, and layer them between parchment so they don't stick together. Crunchy cookies and soft cookies shouldn't be stored in the same container; the crisp ones will absorb the moisture from the others and lose their snap. Most cookies will keep for about three days, though some are best the day of baking, and a few can keep for weeks or even improve over time, such as shortbread and biscotti—if they last that long.

Essential Ingredients

The recipes in this book highlight a diverse array of ingredients. But knowing how to best choose and prepare the fundamentals is the first step to a spectacular cookie.

Butter

In general, we recommend unsalted butter to better control levels of sodium. For some recipes, such as shortbread, use a European-style high-butterfat butter (at least 82%), so its rich flavor shines. When creaming butter and sugar, let the butter come to room temperature—a finger pressed into it should lightly indent it. If you forget to take the butter out of the refrigerator in advance, microwave it in 5-second increments until softened. Or grate it on the large holes of a box grater set over a bowl; it will soften faster than a stick.

Eggs

Eggs are easier to separate when they're cold. But they should be brought to room temperature before using in order to better blend with other ingredients. If you haven't done that, soak them in a bowl of warm water for about 10 minutes.

Sugar

Sugar lends sweetness to dough and provides a caramelized flavor and golden color. Most of our recipes call for granulated sugar. When using brown sugar, pack it into a measuring cup. Confectioners' sugar (finely powdered sugar combined with cornstarch) is a main ingredient in icings and glazes; sift it to remove lumps. Sanding sugar, in fine or coarse grain and various colors, is prized for its sparkle and used for decorating.

Flour

Most of our cookies call for all-purpose flour. We prefer unbleached, as it provides more structure and retains more of the nuances of the wheat. To measure, whisk the flour, then spoon it into a measuring cup and use a knife to level the top, scraping off excess. Add it gradually to the dough, on low speed, and mix until just incorporated, as overmixing results in tougher cookies.

Salt

A small amount of salt balances the sweetness of a cookie and sharpens its flavor. Most recipes call for coarse salt (kosher salt; we like Diamond Crystal), as it dissolves quickly. For sprinkling on top of cookies, use finishing sea salts, such as Maldon or fleur de sel.

Coloring

Food coloring, from natural ingredients like freeze-dried fruit to gel coloring, gives our icings and frostings their beautiful hues. When using gel-paste food coloring, add a drop at a time, or dab a little with a toothpick, and blend well before adding more. Liquid coloring will thin out and dilute the icing or frosting, so add less at first, whisking to combine, and add more if needed.

Chocolate

Our recipes showcase a variety of chocolates, from semisweet or bittersweet, for which we prefer at least 61% cacao, to white. Cocoa powder can be natural or Dutch-process. Natural is untreated and has a pure chocolate flavor; it provides a reddish-brown tone to baked goods. Dutch-process is milder, with a dark, almost black hue when baked.

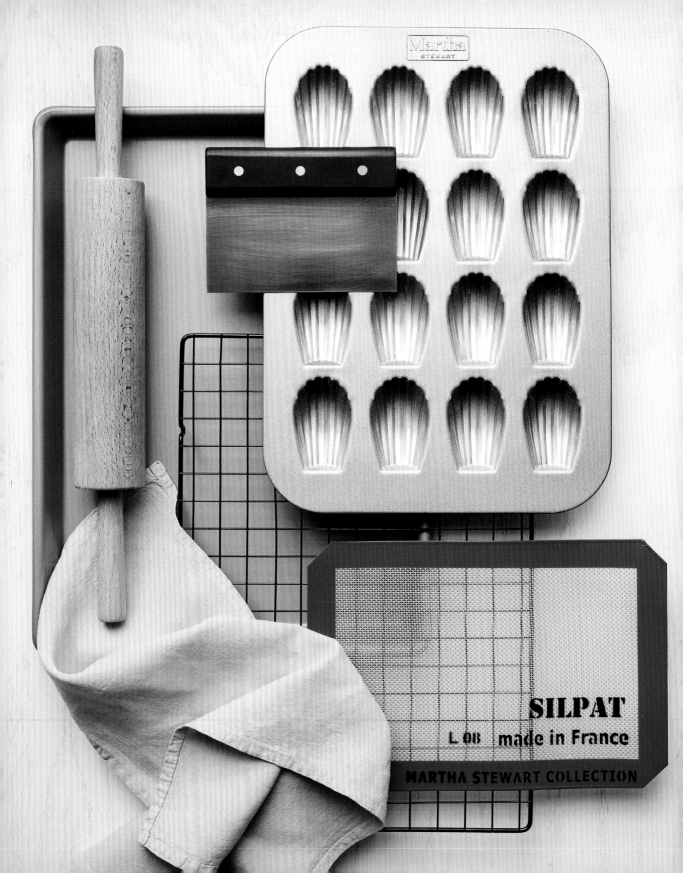

Essential Tools

There are a few tools we just can't live without when it comes to making cookies, and others that significantly quicken and ease the process (think cookie scoop).

Electric mixer

Most of our cookie recipes begin with whisking the dry ingredients, then creaming the butter and sugar—the act of beating room-temperature butter with sugar until pale and fluffy. For this, you'll need an electric mixer. If you're an avid baker, we recommend using a stand mixer, as it blends more evenly and quickly than a hand mixer. (Use the paddle attachment for creaming and the whisk for meringue.) That said, a hand mixer works well for most mixing tasks—including meringue.

Rimmed baking sheets

For even baking, choose heavy-duty aluminum sheets. Rimmed baking sheets have rolled edges, about one inch high, which make them ideal for bar cookies or shortbread. But they suit any kind of cookie, as they'll ensure the dough won't spread beyond the edges. The half-sheet size is about 18 by 13 inches and will fit in a standard oven. Most of our recipes call for at least two baking sheets; let them cool down between batches.

Rolling pin

Rolling pins are essential for evenly rolling dough. There are two kinds of pins, with handles and without (called a French rolling pin). The handled pins are heavy, with a wider diameter, whereas the French are lighter, longer, and more slender. Whichever one you choose, go for a rolling pin made of smooth wood, such as maple, beech, or ash.

Wire racks

Also known as cooling racks, they allow air to circulate around baked cookies (racks with feet encourage airflow). They are also useful for decorating, as they allow excess icing or melted chocolate to drip; line the baking sheet with parchment for easy cleanup. Choose a large, rectangular, stainless-steel rack that will sit comfortably on a baking sheet.

Bench scraper

This versatile kitchen tool loosens and cleans dough from a work surface, and helps transfer chopped ingredients from a cutting board into a bowl. Bench scrapers are made of plastic or stainless steel. Some even come with a ruled edge, doubling as a ruler.

Molds

While most of our cookies require only a baking sheet, some call for a cake pan, a madeleine pan, a waffle-cone maker, or a skillet. Those recipes will have you rethinking the molds in your kitchen, all the while stretching the shape and scope of your cookies.

Parchment and silicone baking mats

We recommend lining your baking sheets with parchment or silicone baking mats. Parchment is better for crisp-bottomed cookies such as Mighty Australian Ginger Cookies (page 126), whereas a mat is good for thin, delicate cookies such as Birch Bark Tuiles (page 36). To clean a mat, simply wipe it with a damp sponge and dry it directly on the rack in a warm oven for a few minutes.

Piping bag

A piping bag, also known as a pastry bag, is a key tool for piping dough and decorating cookies with icing. It consists of a plastic pastry bag that is the shape of a cone and tips of different shapes and sizes, along with couplers to hold the tips securely in place. In a pinch, you can make a pastry bag with parchment paper or a resealable plastic bag.

Tweezers

The perfect tool for precision when placing delicate adornments such as sugared mint leaves, nonpareils, or candy sequins.

Ruler

We use a 12-inch ruler for measuring the diameter of cookies, the size of a scoop, or the space between cookies on a baking sheet. Rulers also come in handy for creating smooth logs of dough for slice-and-bake cookies (see page 240).

Fine-mesh sieve

Also called strainers, sieves come in many sizes. The fine-mesh screen traps small particles, making it ideal for sifting flour or confectioners' sugar to remove lumps. A small sieve can be used to dust cookies with confectioners' sugar. Choose a stainless-steel option.

Spatulas

A large, flat spatula allows you to transfer cookies from a baking sheet to a wire rack, especially the supersized treats in our Giant Cookies chapter (page 115). A small offset spatula is indispensable for spreading icing, and can also be used to smooth the top of shortbread.

Cookie cutters

Cookie cutters are a much-loved and easy-to-use tool for creating different shapes, from simple hearts to ornate animal shapes. Make sure the dough is always well chilled and dip the cutters in flour to prevent the dough from sticking to the cutter.

Cookie scoops

For the neatest and most consistently sized cookies, we like to use a cookie scoop, also known as an ice cream scoop. First, make sure the dough is firm enough to hold its shape. If it's too sticky, simply refrigerate for a few minutes. Keep a few different sizes on hand, from a 1-inch scoop for small thumbprint cookies to a 2¾-inch scoop for the bigger creations in the Giant Cookies chapter.

Pastry brushes

Use a dry pastry brush for wiping excess flour from a work surface or from rolled-out dough. A 1- to 1½-inch brush is just right for brushing cookies with egg wash or glazes.

Tools for texture

We've looked beyond cookie cutters for surprising tools, many of which give our cookies gorgeous textured surfaces. Use the intricate design of a crocheted doily for Glazed Spiced Snowflakes (page 206) and the pointy ridges of a meat mallet for Iranian Rice Cookies (page 151). Embossed mats and rolling pins provide whimsical imprints.

1
ALL DRESSED UP

Trading in the everyday for something
far more special, these cookies take it to the
next level in shape, color, and flavor.
They're frosted, dusted, swirled, and embellished—
thoroughly dressed to impress.

Pastel Butter Cookies

MAKES 40

To give a batch of almond shortbread cookies the pastel treatment, dust them with tinted confectioners' sugar. We blended the sugar with finely ground freeze-dried fruits (blueberry, raspberry, and mango) for subtle, all-natural hues.

1 cup whole blanched almonds, toasted (see page 248)

2 cups unbleached all-purpose flour

½ teaspoon coarse salt

½ teaspoon ground cinnamon

2 sticks (1 cup) unsalted butter, room temperature

1 cup confectioners' sugar, sifted, plus ½ cup per tinted sugar

1 teaspoon vanilla extract

Freeze-dried fruits in various colors, such as blueberries, raspberries, and mangoes

1. Preheat oven to 350°F. Place toasted almonds in the bowl of a food processor. Add flour, salt, and cinnamon, and process until nuts are finely ground, about 1 minute.

2. In a medium bowl, with an electric mixer on medium, beat butter and 1 cup confectioners' sugar until pale and fluffy, about 4 minutes. Add vanilla and beat until combined. With mixer on low, gradually add almond mixture and beat until just incorporated.

3. Using a 1½-inch (1-tablespoon) cookie scoop, drop dough onto parchment-lined baking sheets, spacing about 1 inch apart. Bake cookies, rotating sheets halfway through, until edges are just golden, 14 to 16 minutes. Transfer sheets to wire racks and let cool completely.

4. For each desired color, place ½ cup fruit with ½ cup confectioners' sugar in the bowl of a food processor; process until smooth and evenly tinted. (Sugars can be stored in airtight containers up to 1 month.) Place tinted sugars in small bowls and dip cookies, domed-side down, into tinted sugars to coat. Transfer to a plate and let rest, about 30 minutes. (Cookies can be stored in an airtight container at room temperature up to 1 week.)

TIP

We used pastel powdered food coloring from freeze-dried fruits (found in the snack section of large grocery stores) to decorate these cookies, but for a broader palette of colors, look for the array of pastel powdered sugars at specialty baking stores.

Flower-Embellished Wreaths

MAKES ABOUT 16

Sugar cookies make an elegant statement when dressed up with a simple glaze and a fanciful combination of sugared flowers, candied citrus and ginger, and chopped pistachios. Sicilian pistachios are worth seeking out. Compared with their California cousins, they're smaller, more deeply green with hints of royal purple, and more intensely flavored.

FOR THE COOKIES

2 cups unbleached all-purpose flour, plus more for dusting

¼ teaspoon coarse salt

¼ teaspoon baking powder

1 stick (½ cup) unsalted butter, room temperature

1 cup sugar

½ teaspoon vanilla extract

1 large egg, room temperature

Finely grated zest of 1 orange (about 1 tablespoon)

2 tablespoons brandy

Lemon Glaze (page 246)

TOPPINGS (OPTIONAL)

Candied ginger, finely chopped (see page 248)

Candied citrus, finely chopped (see page 248)

Pistachios (preferably Sicilian), finely chopped

Sugared flowers, such as small pansies, rose petals, and violets (see page 248)

1. Make the cookies: In a medium bowl, whisk together flour, salt, and baking powder. In a large bowl, with an electric mixer on medium-high, beat butter, sugar, and vanilla until pale and fluffy, about 3 minutes. Beat in egg, orange zest, and brandy until well combined. Gradually add flour mixture and mix on low until just combined. On a lightly floured surface, shape dough into a disk, wrap in plastic, and refrigerate until firm, at least 45 minutes and up to overnight.

2. On a lightly floured surface, roll out dough ¼ inch thick. Cut out shapes using a 3½-inch fluted round. Use a 1-inch round cutter to cut out centers of cookies. Reroll scraps once. Transfer wreaths to parchment-lined baking sheets, about 1 inch apart. Refrigerate until firm, at least 1 hour.

3. Preheat oven to 350°F. Bake cookies, rotating sheets halfway through, until set and golden around edges, 15 to 20 minutes. Transfer baking sheets to wire racks and let cool completely.

4. Decorate the cookies: Place lemon glaze in a shallow bowl. Working with one cookie at a time, dip cookie top side down in lemon glaze to coat surface, allowing excess glaze to drip back into bowl. Transfer glazed cookies to a wire rack or baking sheet. Working quickly before glaze sets, use tweezers to decorate cookies with toppings, if desired. Let stand at room temperature until completely dry, at least 2 hours. (Cookies can be stored in an airtight container at room temperature up to overnight.)

Ombré Cookies

Color your buttercream boldly or subtly or countless shades in between for a photo-ready ombré display. Just start with one hue and add a bit of plain white butter-cream for a lighter tone. Instead of using traditional food coloring, we played with plant-based food dye powders for colors that are natural as well as beautiful (see Tip).

2 cups unbleached all-purpose flour, plus more for dusting

½ teaspoon baking powder

¼ teaspoon coarse salt

1 stick (½ cup) unsalted butter, room temperature

1 cup sugar

1 large egg

1 teaspoon vanilla extract

Basic Buttercream (page 245)

Natural food coloring, such as McCormick's Berry and Sunflower

1. In a medium bowl, whisk together flour, baking powder, and salt. In a large bowl, with an electric mixer on medium, beat butter with sugar until pale and fluffy, 3 to 5 minutes. Beat in egg and vanilla until combined. Gradually add flour mixture and mix on low until combined. Divide dough in half and flatten into disks. Wrap each in plastic and freeze until firm, at least 20 minutes, or place in a resealable plastic bag and freeze up to 3 months (thaw in refrigerator overnight before using).

2. Preheat oven to 325°F. Remove one disk of dough; let stand 5 to 10 minutes. Roll dough out ⅛ inch thick between 2 sheets of lightly floured parchment. Cut out shapes with a 2½-inch round cookie cutter. Using a spatula, transfer to parchment-lined baking sheets. (If dough gets soft, refrigerate 10 minutes.) Reroll scraps; cut more shapes.

Repeat with remaining dough. Bake cookies, rotating sheets halfway through, until edges are golden, 10 to 12 minutes. Transfer cookies to wire racks and let cool completely.

3. Place ½ cup buttercream in each of four small bowls. Tint with desired color and let stand 10 minutes to allow dyes to fully saturate. Frost a few cookies with tinted buttercream, using an offset spatula, then add a couple tablespoons white buttercream to each bowl to lighten the colors. Continue frosting cookies, adding more white buttercream to achieve an ombré effect. Reserve remaining butter-cream for another use. (Cookies can be stored in an airtight container at room temperature up to 3 days.)

TIP

For colors shown, we began with a berry-colored dye (made from beets) and a bright yellow (from turmeric). For bright red: mix ¼ teaspoon berry shade with ⅛ teaspoon yellow. For bright pink: use ¼ teaspoon berry shade. For bright orange: mix ¼ teaspoon yellow with a pinch of berry shade. For bright yellow: use ¼ teaspoon yellow.

Chocolate Shortbread Hearts

MAKES 32

Formed with nested cookie cutters in five graduated sizes, these two-tone hearts fit together like puzzle pieces. This allows you to alternate two doughs—white chocolate and dark chocolate with a hint of espresso—for a striking design.

FOR THE DARK-CHOCOLATE SHORTBREAD

1¾ cups unbleached all-purpose flour, plus more for dusting

⅓ cup unsweetened Dutch-process cocoa powder

1½ teaspoons instant espresso powder

¾ teaspoon coarse salt

2 sticks (1 cup) unsalted butter, room temperature

¾ cup confectioners' sugar, sifted

1 teaspoon vanilla extract

FOR THE WHITE-CHOCOLATE SHORTBREAD

2 cups unbleached all-purpose flour, plus more for dusting

¾ teaspoon coarse salt

1 stick (½ cup) plus 6 tablespoons unsalted butter, room temperature

2 ounces white chocolate, melted (see page 248) and slightly cooled

½ cup confectioners' sugar, sifted

1 teaspoon vanilla extract

1. Make dark-chocolate shortbread: In a bowl, whisk flour, cocoa powder, espresso powder, and salt. In a large bowl, with an electric mixer on medium, beat butter until creamy, about 2 minutes; add sugar and beat until combined, then beat in vanilla. Gradually add flour mixture; mix on low until combined. Wrap dough in plastic, flatten to a 1-inch-thick disk, and refrigerate until firm, at least 1 hour and up to 3 days.

2. Make white-chocolate shortbread: In a bowl, whisk flour and salt. In a large bowl, with an electric mixer on medium, beat butter with white chocolate until creamy; add sugar and beat until combined. Beat in vanilla. Gradually add flour mixture; mix on low until combined. Wrap dough in plastic, flatten to a 1-inch-thick disk, and refrigerate until firm, at least 1 hour and up to 3 days.

3. Remove disks from refrigerator; let stand 10 minutes. Roll out dark-chocolate dough ⅛ inch thick between 2 pieces of lightly floured parchment. Stamp out heart shapes with largest cookie cutter; transfer to a parchment-lined baking sheet. Gather dough scraps, reroll, and stamp out heart shapes with largest cutter; freeze until firm, about 15 minutes. Repeat with white-chocolate dough. Stamp out smaller hearts from larger ones, starting with second-largest cutter and working down to smallest cutter; transfer cutouts to parchment-lined baking sheets. Freeze cutouts until firm, about 15 minutes.

4. Preheat oven to 325°F. Starting with smallest cutouts and working up to largest, fit together dark- and white-chocolate cutouts like puzzle pieces. Arrange completed hearts 1 inch apart on parchment-lined baking sheets. Freeze again until firm. Working in 2 batches, bake cookies, rotating sheets halfway through, until firm, 15 to 18 minutes. Transfer cookies to wire racks and let cool. (Cookies can be stored in an airtight container at room temperature up to 1 week.)

Sparkly Lemon Cookies

MAKES 40

These cakey gems get plenty of flavor from lemon zest. Brushing them first with a sweet lemon glaze allows the coarse sanding sugar to better adhere to the tops, giving the cookies a gentle sparkle. They're tasty, whether dressed up or simply glazed and left unadorned.

2 cups unbleached all-purpose flour

¼ teaspoon coarse salt

1 stick (½ cup) plus 2½ tablespoons unsalted butter, room temperature

½ cup plus 2 tablespoons granulated sugar

3 lemons, zested and juiced (⅓ cup juice)

2 large eggs

¼ cup whole milk

2¾ cups confectioners' sugar, sifted

Coarse sanding sugar, for sprinkling (optional)

1. Preheat oven to 325°F. In a small bowl, whisk together flour and salt. In a large bowl, with an electric mixer on medium, beat butter, granulated sugar, and lemon zest until pale and fluffy, about 10 minutes. Beat in eggs until combined. Gradually add flour mixture and mix on low until just combined. Slowly add milk and beat on medium until a dough forms, about 5 minutes.

2. Transfer dough to a pastry bag fitted with a ½-inch round tip (such as Ateco #806). Pipe 1½-inch rounds onto parchment-lined baking sheets. Bake, rotating sheets halfway through, until bottoms of cookies are pale golden, 16 to 18 minutes. Transfer sheets to wire racks and let cool completely.

3. In a bowl, whisk together confectioners' sugar and lemon juice until smooth. Using a pastry brush, brush glaze on cookies. Sprinkle with sanding sugar. Let glaze harden, about 20 minutes. (Cookies can be stored in an airtight container at room temperature for up to 3 days.)

TIP

Feel free to mix up the citrus to use what you have on hand: You can substitute limes for lemons, or use a combination.

Espresso Doily Cookies

MAKES ABOUT 2 DOZEN

These patterned cookies look as intricate, pale, and delicate as snowflakes, yet include the full-bodied flavor of espresso. You can achieve the doily effect with aspic cutters—essentially, tiny cookie cutters that can also shape jellies (cutters, such as the Ateco brand, are available online and in kitchen-supply stores). For gifting, nestle a batch of these lacy sweets in a tin lined with their paper counterparts.

2 tablespoons espresso beans, crushed (see Tip)

¼ cup whole milk

1½ sticks (¾ cup) unsalted butter, room temperature

½ cup confectioners' sugar, sifted, plus more for dusting

½ teaspoon vanilla extract

1 teaspoon coffee extract

2 cups unbleached all-purpose flour, plus more for dusting

½ teaspoon coarse salt

1. In a small saucepan, heat espresso beans and milk over medium-high until milk begins to simmer. Remove from heat and let stand for 15 minutes. Strain through a fine-mesh sieve and discard espresso beans.

2. Meanwhile, in a large bowl, with an electric mixer on medium, beat butter and sugar until pale and fluffy, about 2 minutes. Add both extracts and beat to combine. In a small bowl, whisk together flour and salt. Add flour mixture in 2 additions, alternating with espresso-infused milk, mixing just until dough forms. Shape into a disk, wrap in plastic, and refrigerate at least 30 minutes and up to 2 days.

3. Preheat oven to 325°F. Divide dough in half. On lightly floured parchment, roll out each piece slightly thicker than ⅛ inch. Using scallop-edged or fluted round cutters, cut out cookies and transfer to a baking sheet, spacing about 1 inch apart. Freeze until firm, about 10 minutes.

4. Remove from freezer. Cut out doily patterns in centers of cookies using aspic cutters. (If dough begins to soften, return cookies to freezer until firm.) Gather scraps, shape into a disk, and chill in refrigerator before rerolling and cutting.

5. Bake cookies, rotating sheets halfway through, until edges are set, 12 to 15 minutes. Let cool 5 minutes on baking sheets, then transfer to wire racks to let cool completely. Sift confectioners' sugar over top. (Cookies can be stored in an airtight container at room temperature up to 5 days.)

TIP

To crush espresso beans, place in a resealable bag and gently pound with a heavy skillet, meat mallet, or rolling pin. Alternatively, coarsely grind in a spice grinder or with a mortar and pestle.

Chocolate Mint Wafers

MAKES ABOUT 50

If you can't pass a Girl Scout cookie sale without stocking up on boxes and boxes of minty chocolate wafers, just wait until you try this homemade version. We topped some of the cookies with white nonpareils—reminiscent of the old-fashioned candy—and others with sugared mint leaves.

1 cup unbleached all-purpose flour, plus more for dusting

½ cup unsweetened Dutch-process cocoa powder

¼ teaspoon baking powder

Coarse salt

6 tablespoons unsalted butter, room temperature

½ cup sugar

1 large egg, room temperature

½ teaspoon vanilla extract

12 ounces semisweet or bittersweet chocolate, finely chopped

¼ teaspoon peppermint extract

White nonpareils and sugared mint leaves (see page 248), for decorating (optional)

1. In a medium bowl, whisk together flour, cocoa powder, baking powder, and ¼ teaspoon salt. In a large bowl, with an electric mixer on medium-high, beat butter and sugar until pale and fluffy, about 2 minutes. Beat in egg and vanilla until combined. Gradually add flour mixture and mix on low until just combined. Cover with plastic wrap, and chill at least 1 hour and up to overnight (dough will be very soft).

2. Preheat oven to 350°F. Shape dough into balls (each equal to 1 teaspoon) and transfer to 2 parchment-lined baking sheets, spacing about 2 inches apart. Dip the bottom of a glass in flour and flatten balls into 1½-inch rounds (about ¼ inch thick). Bake cookies, rotating sheets halfway through, until slightly firm to the touch, 8 to 10 minutes. Transfer cookies to wire racks and let cool completely.

3. In a large heatproof bowl set over (not in) a medium pot of simmering water, combine chocolate, peppermint extract, and ⅛ teaspoon salt. Heat, stirring occasionally, until smooth, 2 to 3 minutes; remove from heat.

4. Holding each cookie across the tines of a fork, dip in chocolate to coat completely, then tap underside of fork on side of the bowl to allow excess chocolate to drip off. Transfer to a fresh parchment-lined sheet and repeat until all cookies are coated. Sprinkle some cookies with nonpareils and, using tweezers, place sugared mint leaves in center of others, if desired. Refrigerate until chocolate has set, at least 1 hour. (Cookies can be refrigerated in an airtight container up to 3 days.)

Birch Bark Tuiles

MAKES 2 DOZEN

For a "bark" that is as delicious as its bite, try these crisp, airy cookies, which take on the appearance of birch bark, courtesy of a touch of cocoa powder added to the batter. To achieve the most uniform curled shapes, create a basic stencil (see Tip).

2 large egg whites

½ cup sugar

½ cup unbleached all-purpose flour

¼ teaspoon coarse salt

2½ tablespoons unsalted butter, melted and cooled

4½ teaspoons heavy cream

¼ teaspoon vanilla extract

1 tablespoon unsweetened Dutch-process cocoa powder

1. Line baking sheets with nonstick silicone baking mats (parchment doesn't work as well). In a large bowl, with an electric mixer on medium, beat egg whites with sugar until foamy. Add flour and salt; beat to combine. Add melted butter, cream, and vanilla, and beat to combine.

2. Transfer ½ cup batter to a small bowl and stir in cocoa powder. Transfer to a pastry bag fitted with a small round tip (such as Ateco #3 or #4). Pipe small dots and dashes and "knots" sparsely across surface of baking mats, mimicking the texture of birch bark; you can also use a paintbrush. Freeze 15 minutes.

3. Preheat oven to 325°F. Place stencil over "birch" markings (see Tip); spoon about 1½ teaspoons batter into stencil. Spread evenly with a small offset spatula (it will be very thin, and it's okay if some of the markings smear). Repeat to fill baking sheet (about 6 per sheet). Remove stencil and bake cookies until just set and barely golden on edges, 8 to 9 minutes. Let cool 30 seconds.

4. Working with one cookie at a time, loosen edges with a spatula and remove from pan. Roll cookies into cylinders and place, seam side down, on a tray. (Return cookies to oven for a few seconds to warm if they start to get brittle before you roll them.) Once cookies are shaped, let cool completely.

5. Clean baking mats and stencil between batches, and repeat with remaining batter. (Cookies can be stored in an airtight container at room temperature up to 3 days.)

TIP

To make a stencil: Trace a 5-inch circle on a piece of heavy plastic (such as the top of a take-out container). Then trace a 3½-inch circle in the center. Cut out both circles with a utility knife, creating an O stencil.

Animal Gingerbread Cookies

MAKES ABOUT FIFTY 3- TO 4-INCH COOKIES

Create wild things in gingerbread, with a gathering of farm and forest creatures that spring to life with features piped in royal icing. Piping can be as easy as the polar bear's solid white with dots for an eye and nose (a good one for kids), or as fancy as the fox's fur and the sheep's fluffy wool.

5½ cups unbleached all-purpose flour, plus more for dusting

1 teaspoon baking soda

1½ teaspoons coarse salt

4 teaspoons ground ginger

4 teaspoons ground cinnamon

1 teaspoon freshly grated nutmeg

1½ teaspoons ground cloves

2 sticks (1 cup) unsalted butter, room temperature

1 cup packed dark brown sugar

2 large eggs, room temperature

1½ cups unsulfured molasses

4 cups Royal Icing (page 244)

Brown and black gel-paste food coloring

Fine sanding and pearl sugars, for decorating

---

1. In a large bowl, whisk together flour, baking soda, salt, ginger, cinnamon, nutmeg, and cloves. In another large bowl, with an electric mixer on medium-high, beat butter and brown sugar until fluffy, 2 to 3 minutes. Beat in eggs, one at a time, then molasses. Gradually add flour mixture and mix on low until just combined. Shape dough into 3 disks, and wrap each in plastic. Refrigerate until firm but still pliable, about 1 hour.

2. Working with one disk of dough at a time, roll out to ¼-inch thickness on generously floured parchment. Brush off excess flour, transfer dough on parchment to a baking sheet, and freeze until firm, about 15 minutes. Cut out desired shapes with cookie cutters, rerolling scraps. Transfer cookies to parchment-lined baking sheets and freeze until firm, about 15 minutes.

3. Preheat oven to 350°F. Bake cookies until edges turn golden, about 15 minutes, rotating once and firmly rapping baking sheet halfway through to flatten any bubbles. Transfer sheets to wire racks and let cookies cool completely.

4. Divide icing into batches (set aside ½ cup), and mix in a different shade of food coloring to each to tint. Transfer brown and white royal icing to two pastry bags fitted with small round tips (Ateco #1 or #2). Flood cookies with icing (see page 243), using dark brown for reindeer, light brown for foxes, and white for sheep, cows, and polar bears. Sprinkle white cookies with sanding sugar for polar bears, and pearl sugar for sheep. Tap off excess. Let icing set at room temperature overnight.

5. Add confectioners' sugar to reserved icing, one tablespoon at a time, to reach consistency of toothpaste. Tint with desired food coloring (black for eyes, brown for spots and fur). Transfer to pastry bags fitted with small round tips or a closed star tip (Ateco #13) for foxes. Decorate as desired. Let set overnight. (Cookies can be stored in an airtight container at room temperature up to 1 week.)

Vanilla–Chocolate Log Cookies

MAKES ABOUT 3 DOZEN

Inspired by the rings of a gracefully aged tree, this shortbread cookie contains two flavors of dough swirled into a single log. Give the edges of the baked cookies a quick dip in chocolate ("bark") and chopped pistachio ("moss") for extra woodsy appeal.

2 cups unbleached all-purpose flour

1 teaspoon coarse salt

2 sticks (1 cup) unsalted butter, room temperature

1½ cups confectioners' sugar, sifted

1 teaspoon vanilla extract

3 tablespoons unsweetened Dutch-process cocoa powder

½ teaspoon instant espresso powder

2 tablespoons hot water

3 ounces milk chocolate, melted (see page 248)

¼ cup finely chopped pistachios

1. In a medium bowl, whisk together flour and salt. In a large bowl, with an electric mixer on medium, beat butter, sugar, and vanilla until pale and fluffy, about 2 minutes. Gradually add flour mixture and mix on low until just combined. Remove half the dough; divide into 2 equal pieces, shape into disks, wrap in plastic, and set aside while you make the chocolate dough.

2. In a small bowl, stir together cocoa powder, espresso, and hot water. Add cocoa mixture to remaining cookie dough and mix on low until color is uniform, scraping down sides of bowl as needed. Place half the chocolate dough on a sheet of parchment and cover with plastic wrap. Roll dough into a 10-by-14-inch rectangle (dough will be very thin but can be easily patched if it tears); reserve. Repeat with remaining chocolate dough and both pieces of vanilla dough.

3. Place one sheet of chocolate dough on work surface and remove plastic. Remove plastic from one sheet of vanilla dough and invert, still attached to its parchment backing, onto chocolate dough, pressing gently with the palm of your hand to adhere. Gently peel back parchment to remove. Continue layering with remaining chocolate and vanilla doughs. With a short side close to you, roll dough into a tight spiral. Wrap in parchment and place in a paper-towel tube (see page 240). Refrigerate until firm, at least 1 hour and up to overnight.

4. Preheat oven to 325°F. Trim ends from dough. Slice dough ¼ inch thick. Roll each cookie between sheets of parchment into an oblong disk about 3 inches long and ⅛ inch thick; transfer to 2 parchment-lined sheets.

5. Bake cookies until crisp, 8 to 10 minutes. Transfer sheets to wire racks and let cool completely. Working with one cookie at a time, dip an edge in melted chocolate and coat with pistachios. Transfer to fresh parchment-lined baking sheets and let stand until chocolate is set, 45 to 60 minutes. (Cookies can be stored in an airtight container at room temperature up to 5 days.)

PERFECTING
SWISS MERINGUES

With Swiss meringue's light-as-a-feather consistency, you can see why cookies made from it are named after ethereal kisses and clouds, and piped accordingly. Sugar is the essence of meringue, stabilizing the whipped egg whites and giving structure to the fragile foam, allowing it to hold its shape. The three recipes on the following page use a similar base (below), but play with ingredients to make one simply white and dipped in coconut, one candy-striped, and another fruit-kissed and pale pink.

MAKES 1 DOZEN

8 large egg whites

1¼ cups sugar

2 teaspoons cornstarch

2 teaspoons vanilla extract

1. Preheat oven to 300°F. Place egg whites and sugar in the large heatproof bowl of an electric mixer. Set bowl over (not in) a medium pot of simmering water and cook, whisking frequently, until sugar dissolves and mixture is just hot to the touch, about 3 minutes.

2. With an electric mixer on high (use whisk attachment if using a stand mixer), whisk egg whites and sugar mixture until stiff, glossy peaks form, about 5 minutes. Add cornstarch and vanilla and whisk until combined.

3. Place a small dab of meringue on each corner of a baking sheet, underneath a sheet of parchment, to hold it in place. Pipe or spoon meringue onto parchment (see variations on page 44), spacing about 1 inch apart.

4. Transfer meringues to oven and immediately lower the temperature to 200°F. Bake until firm but still pliable, about 30 minutes. Turn off oven and allow meringues to continue drying 2 hours and up to overnight. (Meringues can be stored in an airtight container in a cool, dry place up to 2 weeks.)

White-Chocolate Swiss Meringue Kisses

MAKES 3 DOZEN

Prepare a pastry bag fitted with a ½-inch plain round tip (such as Ateco #806). Prepare Swiss meringue through step 2, adding 1 teaspoon vanilla extract (instead of 2 teaspoons) and seeds from 1 vanilla bean to the egg whites and sugar mixture when adding cornstarch. Prepare sheet as in step 3. Transfer mixture to prepared piping bag. Pipe 1-inch-diameter kisses, spacing about 1 inch apart, on baking sheets. Bake as directed in step 4. When cool, dip bottom of each meringue in 8 ounces white chocolate, melted (see page 248), followed by 1 cup unsweetened shredded coconut. Transfer to a wire rack. Allow to set at room temperature, about 30 minutes.

Raspberry Swiss Meringue Clouds

MAKES 1 DOZEN

Place ¼ cup freeze-dried raspberries in the bowl of a food processor and process until finely powdered. Pass through a fine-mesh sieve to remove seeds; set aside. Prepare Swiss meringue through step 2. Gently fold in raspberries and 2 to 3 drops soft-pink gel food coloring (or more as needed to reach desired shade). Prepare sheet as in step 3. Using a small spoon, drop mounds of meringue, about 3 inches in diameter, on parchment-lined sheets, spacing about 1 inch apart. Bake as directed in step 4.

Candy-Striped Swiss Meringue Kisses

MAKES 2 DOZEN

Prepare a pastry bag with a ½-inch open-star tip (such as Ateco #826). Using a small brush, paint 3 evenly spaced stripes of soft-pink gel food coloring inside the piping bag, starting at the tip and ending about 4 inches below the top of the bag. Prepare Swiss meringue through step 2, and prepare sheet as in step 3. Transfer mixture to prepared piping bag. Pipe 2-inch-diameter swirls, about 1 inch apart, on baking sheets. Bake as directed in step 4.

Tips for Meringue

● To keep the meringue from breaking, always use a spotlessly clean mixing bowl. Rinse the bowl out with hot water and a drop of lemon juice, then rinse it well and dry completely.

● To test for undissolved sugar, rub a bit of the warming egg-white mixture between your fingers. When you can't feel granules of sugar, the mixture is ready for the next step.

● Create a strong meringue by using a low speed on your mixer and gradually increasing the speed to high. This enables many smaller air bubbles to form, instead of fewer large ones.

● Meringue batter is ready when you remove the beater from the bowl, invert it, and peaks of meringue gently tip over.

● To hold the parchment in place on your baking sheets, pipe a small dab of meringue batter beneath each corner of the parchment.

2

CLASSICS WITH A TWIST

Just when you think a tried-and-true cookie couldn't possibly be more perfect, it is: green-tea shortbread, a carrot-cake thumbprint, spiced-chocolate biscotti, and more. We've reimagined our best-loved favorites by channeling those familiar flavors and shapes into new, even more delicious iterations.

Potato Chip Cookies

MAKES ABOUT 18

Everybody's favorite salty snack takes a walk on the sweet side, turning a traditional rolled cookie into a crunchy, chewy, addictive treat. We kept it simple, but no doubt adding chocolate chips would make someone's day. Prepare the dough just before you plan to bake the cookies, as refrigerating it may cause the potato chips to get soggy.

2¼ cups unbleached all-purpose flour

1 teaspoon baking soda

¾ teaspoon coarse salt

2 sticks (1 cup) unsalted butter, room temperature

¾ cup packed light brown sugar

¾ cup granulated sugar

1 teaspoon vanilla extract

2 large eggs

4 cups coarsely crushed salted potato chips (about 10 ounces)

1 cup pecans, toasted (see page 248) and coarsely chopped

1. Preheat oven to 375°F. In a medium bowl, whisk together flour, baking soda, and salt. In a large bowl, with an electric mixer on high, beat butter and both sugars until pale and fluffy, 2 to 3 minutes. Add vanilla and eggs, and beat on medium until just combined. Gradually add flour mixture and beat on low until just combined. Stir in 2 cups potato chips and the nuts.

2. Place remaining potato chips in a shallow bowl. Scoop 2-inch tablespoons of dough and roll into balls; then roll in potato chips to coat. Transfer cookies to parchment-lined baking sheets, spacing about 2 inches apart.

3. Bake, rotating sheets halfway through, until golden, 18 to 20 minutes. Transfer sheets to wire racks and let cool completely. (Cookies can be stored in an airtight container at room temperature up to 5 days.)

TIP

For chocolate-chip-cookie fans, stir in 2 cups chocolate chips when adding the potato chips and nuts in step 1.

Pumpkin Snickerdoodles

MAKES ABOUT 2 DOZEN

Sugar and spice aren't the only things nice in this version of the beloved snickerdoodle: Pumpkin puree infuses the cookies with seasonal flavor and helps to create a moist, cakey center. Starting the dough with melted (rather than softened) butter gives them a delightful chew. And rolling them in spiced sanding sugar just before baking lends sparkle and shine.

2 cups unbleached all-purpose flour

½ teaspoon baking soda

½ teaspoon cream of tartar

½ teaspoon coarse salt

Pinch of freshly grated nutmeg

1 stick (½ cup) unsalted butter, melted and cooled

1 cup granulated sugar

½ cup canned pumpkin puree (not pie filling)

1 large egg, room temperature

1 teaspoon vanilla extract

⅓ cup fine sanding sugar

1 teaspoon ground cinnamon

½ teaspoon ground allspice

1. Preheat oven to 375°F. In a medium bowl, whisk together flour, baking soda, cream of tartar, salt, and nutmeg. In a large bowl, whisk together butter, granulated sugar, and pumpkin until smooth. Add egg and vanilla and whisk to combine. Gradually add flour mixture and stir to combine, about 2 minutes.

2. In a small bowl, whisk together sanding sugar, cinnamon, and allspice. Scoop tablespoons of dough and roll into 1½-inch balls; roll in sugar mixture. Transfer to parchment-lined baking sheets, spacing each about 3 inches apart. Using the bottom of a glass, flatten balls to just under ½ inch thick. Sprinkle with more sugar mixture.

3. Bake cookies, rotating sheets halfway through, until light golden and firm to touch, 10 to 12 minutes. Let cool 5 minutes on sheets, then transfer to a wire rack and let cool completely. (Cookies can be stored in an airtight container at room temperature up to 3 days.)

Carrot-Cake Thumbprint Cookies

MAKES 18

Carrot cake gets reinvented as dreamy bites: Grated carrots, chopped pecans, plump golden raisins, and rolled oats form a textured base for these cakey thumbprints. To make the creamy filling, we substituted the usual cream cheese with goat cheese, then swirled in apricot jam.

1 stick (½ cup) unsalted butter, melted, plus 4 tablespoons, room temperature, for filling

⅓ cup packed light brown sugar

⅓ cup granulated sugar

1 large egg yolk

1 cup unbleached all-purpose flour

½ teaspoon ground ginger

½ teaspoon ground cinnamon

¾ teaspoon coarse salt

¾ cup old-fashioned rolled oats

¾ cup packed finely grated carrots (about 3 medium)

¼ cup golden raisins, chopped

¾ cup pecans, finely chopped

¼ cup confectioners' sugar, sifted

2 ounces fresh goat cheese, room temperature

1½ teaspoons apricot jam

1. Preheat oven to 350°F. In a large bowl, whisk together melted butter, brown and granulated sugars, and egg yolk. In a medium bowl, whisk together flour, ginger, cinnamon, and salt. Stir flour mixture into butter mixture to combine. Mix in oats, carrots, and raisins. Cover and refrigerate 30 minutes.

2. Scoop dough and roll 1½-inch balls; then roll balls in pecans to coat. Transfer to parchment-lined baking sheets, spacing about 2 inches apart.

3. Bake 10 minutes. Remove from oven and press an indentation into center of each cookie with the end of a wooden spoon. Continue to bake until golden brown on bottom, 10 to 12 minutes more. Transfer cookies to a wire rack and let cool completely.

4. In a medium bowl, with an electric mixer on medium, beat remaining 4 tablespoons butter and confectioners' sugar until smooth. Beat in goat cheese until just combined. Swirl in jam. Pipe or spoon goat-cheese mixture into center. (Cookies can be refrigerated in an airtight container for 3 days.)

Linzer Flower Cookies

MAKES 1 DOZEN

The classic Linzer torte, with its mouthwatering combination of buttery hazelnuts and fruity jam, has been reimagined in these mini blooming versions. Black currant jelly is traditionally used, but we love the bright flavors and hues of berry jams and orange marmalade. Petal-shaped cookie cutters let those colors shine through.

1 cup blanched hazelnuts, toasted (see page 248)

2 sticks (1 cup) unsalted butter, room temperature

½ cup granulated sugar

1 large egg, room temperature

1 teaspoon vanilla extract

2 cups plus 2 tablespoons unbleached all-purpose flour, plus more for dusting

1 teaspoon baking powder

1 teaspoon ground cinnamon

½ teaspoon coarse salt

¼ teaspoon freshly grated nutmeg

Confectioners' sugar, for dusting

¼ cup berry jam, such as raspberry

¼ cup orange marmalade

1. Pulse hazelnuts in a food processor until finely ground.

2. In a large bowl, with an electric mixer on medium, beat butter and granulated sugar until pale and fluffy, about 2 minutes. Add egg and beat until smooth. Beat in vanilla.

3. In a medium bowl, whisk together ground hazelnuts, flour, baking powder, cinnamon, salt, and nutmeg. Add to butter mixture and beat on low until just combined. Divide dough in half, shape each half into a disk, and wrap in plastic. Refrigerate until firm, at least 1 hour and up to overnight.

4. Preheat oven to 350°F. On lightly floured parchment, roll out one disk of dough ¼ inch thick. Using a 3½-inch flower-shaped cutter, cut out cookies. (If dough is too soft, freeze 10 minutes.) Using a large spatula, transfer to parchment-lined baking sheets. Using a ¾-inch petal-shaped cutter, cut out centers of petals from half the cookies. Repeat process with remaining disk of dough. Gather scraps from both disks, reroll, and cut.

5. Place cookie tops (with cutouts) on one baking sheet and bottoms (solid cookies) on the other. The thinner, more fragile tops will bake more quickly, and may need to be removed from the oven before the bottoms are finished baking. Bake cookies, rotating halfway through, until edges are slightly golden, 12 to 14 minutes. Transfer sheets to wire racks and let cool completely.

6. Lightly sift confectioners' sugar over cookies with cutout petals. Spread a heaping teaspoon of jam on each solid cookie and carefully sandwich with sugared cookies. (Unfilled cookies can be stored in an airtight container at room temperature up to 2 days. Fill with preserves just before serving.)

Molasses-Ginger Crisps

MAKES 8 DOZEN

A ginger-lover's treat, if ever there was one, and a favorite of Martha's, this crisp includes a trio of gingers—fresh, ground, and crystallized (cooked in syrup and dried)—for a full-spectrum sampler of the spicy root. While baking, these cookies will fill your kitchen with an incredible fragrance, and when it comes time for eating, their bright snap will leave you wanting more.

2 cups plus 2 tablespoons unbleached all-purpose flour

1½ teaspoons ground ginger

1 teaspoon baking soda

¾ teaspoon coarse salt

2 sticks (1 cup) unsalted butter, room temperature

1½ cups granulated sugar

1 large egg, plus 1 large egg yolk, room temperature

2 tablespoons finely chopped crystallized ginger

1 teaspoon finely grated peeled fresh ginger

⅓ cup unsulfured molasses

1 cup coarse sanding sugar

1. In a medium bowl, whisk together flour, ground ginger, baking soda, and salt. In a large bowl, with an electric mixer on medium-high, beat butter and granulated sugar until pale and fluffy, about 2 minutes. Beat in egg and egg yolk, crystallized ginger, and grated ginger. Add flour mixture in 3 additions, alternating with molasses; mix on low until well combined. Cover and refrigerate until firm, at least 1 hour.

2. Preheat oven to 350°F. Using a 1-teaspoon measuring spoon or cookie scoop, scoop dough and roll into balls, then coat with sanding sugar. Transfer to parchment-lined baking sheets, spacing 2 inches apart.

3. Bake, rotating sheets halfway through, until cookies are flat and edges are dark golden brown, 12 to 14 minutes. Let cool 5 minutes on baking sheets. Transfer cookies to wire racks to cool completely. (Cookies can be stored in an airtight container at room temperature up to 2 days or frozen up to a month.)

TIP

The easiest way to peel fresh ginger is to reach for a spoon. It removes the thin skin easily, even from the knotty areas. Hold the spoon, concave side facing you, and draw it toward you. Maneuver the spoon and ginger as necessary to get into all the crevices.

Tahini Cookies

MAKES ABOUT 20

When you're craving a nutty sweet in a stylish package, consider sesame instead of the usual peanut butter. This one gets a double dose of flavor: Tahini—the creamy paste made from ground toasted sesame seeds—contributes to a full-flavored dough, which is then rolled in sesame seeds to give the cookies a satisfying crunch.

1½ cups unbleached all-purpose flour

¾ teaspoon baking soda

½ teaspoon coarse salt

1 stick (½ cup) unsalted butter, room temperature

1 cup sugar

1 large egg, room temperature

1 teaspoon vanilla extract

½ cup tahini, well stirred

½ cup white sesame seeds, or a combination of black and white, lightly toasted

1. In a medium bowl, whisk together flour, baking soda, and salt. In a large bowl, with an electric mixer on medium-high, beat butter, sugar, egg, and vanilla until pale and fluffy, about 2 minutes. Beat in tahini until combined. With mixer on low, beat in flour mixture until just combined. Cover and refrigerate until firm, about 30 minutes.

2. Preheat oven to 350°F. Spread sesame seeds in a shallow dish. Scoop 2 tablespoons of dough and roll into a ball. Roll in sesame seeds until thoroughly coated, then transfer to parchment-lined baking sheets. Repeat with remaining dough, spacing cookies 3 inches apart.

3. Bake cookies, rotating sheets halfway through, until golden brown, 18 to 20 minutes. Transfer sheets to wire racks and let cool completely. (Cookies can be stored in an airtight container at room temperature up to 5 days.)

TIP

Sesame seeds can quickly turn rancid, so buy only small batches. Store them in the refrigerator for up to 3 months or freeze.

Cornmeal Chocolate–Chunk Cookies

MAKES 3 DOZEN

Inspired by the celebrated semolina loaf with golden raisins and fennel seeds at Amy's Bread in New York, our test kitchen developed this cookie (adding chopped milk chocolate for good measure). It's an extraordinary combination of flavors and textures: Cornmeal makes the cookies crisp on the outside, while the raisins yield a chewy bite.

1 tablespoon fennel seeds

1½ sticks (¾ cup) unsalted butter, room temperature

1 cup sugar

1 large egg, room temperature

1 cup unbleached all-purpose flour

⅔ cup medium-grind yellow cornmeal

1 teaspoon baking powder

¾ teaspoon coarse salt

¾ cup golden raisins

5 ounces milk chocolate, coarsely chopped

1. Toast fennel seeds in a small skillet over medium heat until fragrant, about 2 minutes, shaking pan occasionally; let cool. Using a spice grinder or mortar and pestle, finely grind fennel seeds.

2. Preheat oven to 350°F. In a large bowl, with an electric mixer on medium-high, beat butter with sugar and ground fennel until pale and fluffy, about 3 minutes. Beat in egg until combined. Add flour, cornmeal, baking powder, and salt, and beat until just combined. Stir in raisins and chocolate.

3. Scoop heaping tablespoons of dough (or use a 1½-inch ice cream scoop) onto parchment-lined baking sheets, spacing about 2 inches apart. Bake cookies, rotating sheets halfway through, until edges are golden, about 15 minutes. Transfer sheets to wire racks and let cool at least 10 minutes before serving warm or at room temperature. (Cooled completely, cookies can be stored in an airtight container at room temperature up to 3 days.)

TIP

Use a serrated knife to cut the chocolate into chunks. We used milk chocolate here, but dark chocolate would also work nicely.

Brown-Butter Crinkle Cookies

MAKES 3 DOZEN

These little cookies have a nutty undercurrent of brown butter. Their artfully crinkled surfaces are the result of rolling the dough in two kinds of sugar before baking. Granulated sugar helps the confectioners' sugar cling to the surface. As the cookies bake and spread, their surface cracks, creating a zigzag of sugar and dough.

1 stick (½ cup) unsalted butter

2¼ cups unbleached all-purpose flour

¾ teaspoon baking powder

½ teaspoon ground cinnamon

¾ teaspoon coarse salt

1 cup granulated sugar

½ cup packed dark brown sugar

2 large eggs

1 teaspoon vanilla extract

¾ cup confectioners' sugar, sifted

1. Melt butter in a saucepan over medium-high. When it boils, reduce heat to medium; simmer until foamy. Continue cooking, stirring occasionally and scraping bottom of pan, until foam subsides, butter turns golden brown with a nutty aroma, and milk solids separate into brown specks that sink to bottom, 2 to 7 minutes. Remove from heat; transfer to a large heatproof bowl and let cool 10 minutes.

2. Meanwhile, in a medium bowl, whisk together flour, baking powder, cinnamon, and salt. Stir ½ cup of the granulated sugar and the brown sugar into brown butter until combined, then stir in eggs and vanilla. Add flour mixture and stir until a dough forms. Transfer to a piece of plastic wrap, shape into a disk, and wrap tightly. Refrigerate until firm, at least 1 hour and up to 2 days.

3. Preheat oven to 350°F. Place confectioners' sugar and remaining ½ cup granulated sugar in 2 separate bowls. Scoop 1 tablespoon dough and roll into a ball; roll in granulated sugar, then coat with confectioners' sugar (do not shake off excess). Transfer to parchment-lined baking sheets, spacing cookies about 1 inch apart. Repeat with remaining dough and sugars.

4. Bake, rotating sheets halfway through, until cookies spread slightly, crackle, and are set at edges, 15 to 18 minutes. Let cool on sheets on wire racks 5 minutes, then carefully transfer to racks; let cool completely. (Cookies can be stored in an airtight container at room temperature in a single layer up to 2 days.)

Oat-and-Spelt Shortbread

MAKES 16

There's a nuttiness and a lightness to spelt flour that plain wheat flour lacks. Coupled with rolled oats, it makes for a fiber-rich shortbread that's surprisingly tender. We gave our batch a dunk in bittersweet chocolate and a sprinkle of sea salt for a pretty geometric look and an extra dimension of sweetness.

1¼ cups spelt flour, plus more for dusting

1 cup old-fashioned rolled oats

½ teaspoon coarse salt

1 stick (½ cup) unsalted butter, room temperature

½ cup natural cane sugar

1 large egg, room temperature

1 teaspoon vanilla extract

4 ounces bittersweet chocolate, melted (see page 248)

Flaky sea salt, such as Maldon (optional)

1. In a medium bowl, whisk together flour, oats, and coarse salt. In a large bowl, with an electric mixer on high, beat butter with sugar until pale and fluffy, about 3 minutes. Beat in egg and vanilla until combined. Gradually add flour mixture and mix on low until just combined.

2. Gather dough in plastic wrap; form into a rectangle and refrigerate until firm, at least 1 hour and up to 1 day.

3. Preheat oven to 325°F. Roll out dough between lightly floured parchment to a scant ½-inch thickness; cut into 2-inch squares. Transfer to 2 parchment-lined baking sheets, spacing cookies about 1 inch apart. Bake, rotating sheets halfway through, until firm to the touch and golden around edges, 24 to 26 minutes. Let cool completely.

4. Dip each cookie diagonally in chocolate; sprinkle with flaky sea salt, if desired. Transfer to parchment-lined sheets and refrigerate until just set. (Cookies can be refrigerated in an airtight container up to 3 days.)

TIP

Spelt four can be substituted one-to-one for all-purpose or whole-wheat flour in recipes that don't require yeast.

Spicy Chocolate Cookies

MAKES ABOUT 3 DOZEN

With its deep cocoa flavor, smooth texture, and assertive kick of cayenne pepper and cinnamon, this cookie has all the best qualities of Mexican hot chocolate. When baked, the chopped semisweet chocolate melts, producing a velvety interior.

1½ cups unbleached all-purpose flour

¼ cup unsweetened Dutch-process cocoa powder

1 teaspoon ground cinnamon

½ teaspoon coarse salt

¼ teaspoon cayenne pepper

1 teaspoon baking soda

1 stick (½ cup) unsalted butter, room temperature

1 cup packed dark brown sugar

1 large egg, room temperature

1 teaspoon vanilla extract

12 ounces semisweet chocolate, chopped

½ cup turbinado sugar

1. Preheat oven to 325°F. In a medium bowl, whisk together flour, cocoa powder, cinnamon, salt, cayenne, and baking soda.

2. In a large bowl, with an electric mixer on medium-high, beat butter and brown sugar until light and fluffy, about 3 minutes. Beat in egg and vanilla until well combined. Reduce speed to low and beat in flour mixture until just combined. Stir in chocolate.

3. Scoop dough and roll into 1-inch balls. Gently roll in turbinado sugar to coat and place on parchment-lined baking sheets, spacing cookies 2 inches apart.

4. Bake, rotating sheets halfway through, until surfaces crack slightly, 11 to 14 minutes. Let cool 5 minutes on baking sheets, then transfer to wire racks and let cool completely. (Cookies can be stored in an airtight container at room temperature for up to 1 week.)

TIP

Dutch-process cocoa, which has been treated to neutralize its acidity, has a richer, darker color and mellower flavor than regular cocoa. Natural cocoa has a lighter reddish hue. It's a good idea to have both cocoas on hand.

Green Tea Cookies

MAKES ABOUT 7 DOZEN

These cookies boast green tea in two forms: matcha, the green tea powder found in Japanese tea ceremonies, and finely ground tea leaves. We love the fragrant, floral note they bring to these shortbread-like cookies. Matcha—a superfood with a wealth of vitamins and antioxidants—has a flour-like texture that's easily incorporated into baked goods, and it gently tints the shortbread a soft green.

2 cups unbleached all-purpose flour

2 tablespoons finely ground green tea leaves (from about 8 tea bags; see Tip)

1 tablespoon matcha

½ teaspoon salt

2 sticks (1 cup) unsalted butter, room temperature

½ cup plus 2 tablespoons confectioners' sugar, sifted

1. In a medium bowl, whisk together flour, tea leaves, matcha, and salt. In a large bowl, with an electric mixer on medium, beat butter and sugar until pale and fluffy, about 3 minutes. With mixer on low, gradually mix in flour mixture until just combined.

2. Divide dough in half. Transfer each half to a piece of parchment paper; shape into logs 1¼ inches in diameter and wrap in parchment (see Slice-and-Bake Cookies, page 240). Freeze until firm, about 1 hour.

3. Preheat oven to 350°F. Unwrap frozen logs and slice ¼ inch thick. Transfer to parchment-lined baking sheets, spacing each about 1 inch apart. Bake cookies, rotating sheets halfway through, until edges turn golden, 13 to 15 minutes. Transfer baking sheets to wire racks and let cool. (Cookies can be stored in an airtight container at room temperature up to 1 week.)

TIP

You can grind tea leaves in a spice grinder or with a mortar and pestle.

Streusel Jammies

MAKES 2 DOZEN

A ground-almond dough plays a dual role in these crisp jammies: Three-quarters of the dough is pressed into rounds, and the remainder is sprinkled around the jam centers like a streusel. They're inspired by the crumble-topped tart called *torta sbrisolona*, a specialty of Mantua, Italy.

1½ cups blanched almonds

1¾ cups unbleached all-purpose flour

¾ cup sugar

½ teaspoon coarse salt

¼ teaspoon almond extract

1½ sticks (¾ cup) unsalted butter, room temperature

½ cup assorted jams, such as apricot, cranberry, cherry, and blueberry, separately whisked until smooth

1. Finely grind almonds in a food processor. Preheat oven to 350°F. In a large bowl, whisk together ground almonds, flour, sugar, salt, and almond extract. Cut in butter using a pastry blender or 2 forks until completely incorporated.

2. Working directly on 2 parchment-lined baking sheets, firmly press 2 tablespoons dough into the bottom of a 2½-inch round cookie cutter; then gently lift cutter to leave dough on parchment. Repeat, spacing cookies evenly on sheets, until you've made 24 rounds. Dollop 1 teaspoon jam into center of each round, alternating flavors. Sprinkle 1 tablespoon of remaining dough around border of each cookie.

3. Bake cookies, rotating sheets halfway through, until golden brown at the edges, about 24 minutes. Transfer cookies on sheets to wire racks and let cool completely. (Cookies can be stored in an airtight container at room temperature up to 2 days.)

TIP

Made from the oil of the bitter almond, pure almond extract is a great complement to baked goods. A little goes a long way, however, so use it judiciously.

Key Lime Sablés

MAKES ABOUT 80

Sablé, French for "sand," is an accurate name for this shortbread cookie, with its appealingly crisp, sandy texture. We opted for the zest and juice of Florida Key limes to bring a bright shot of flavor to these classic butter cookies. The citrus is more aromatic and floral than the larger, commonly found Persian lime.

1½ cups unbleached all-purpose flour, plus more for dusting

½ teaspoon coarse salt

1½ sticks (¾ cup) unsalted butter, room temperature

1 cup confectioners' sugar, sifted

2 tablespoons finely grated Key lime zest (from about 15 limes)

2 tablespoons fresh Key lime juice (from about 5 limes)

Fine sanding sugar, for decorating (optional)

1. In a medium bowl, whisk together flour and salt. In a large bowl, with an electric mixer on medium-high, beat butter and confectioners' sugar until pale and fluffy, about 3 minutes. Beat in lime zest and juice. Gradually add flour mixture and mix on low until just combined. Divide dough in half, form each half into a disk, and wrap in plastic. Refrigerate until chilled, at least 1 hour and up to overnight.

2. Roll out each portion of dough between lightly floured parchment to ¼ inch thick. Place dough and parchment on baking sheets, and freeze until firm, about 15 minutes.

3. Preheat oven to 325°F. Using a 2-inch fluted cutter, cut out cookies. Reroll scraps and repeat. Using a sharp knife, cut 6 slits into each cookie. Transfer to parchment-lined baking sheets, spacing about 1 inch apart. Freeze until firm, about 15 minutes. Sprinkle with sanding sugar, if desired.

4. Bake cookies, rotating sheets halfway through, until bottoms begin to turn golden brown, 12 to 15 minutes. Transfer sheets to wire racks and let cool slightly. Transfer cookies to racks to cool completely. (Cookies can be stored in an airtight container at room temperature for up to 3 days.)

TIP

You can use regular limes in this recipe (with the same amount of fresh juice), but increase the zest to 2½ tablespoons.

Pink-Lemonade Thumbprints

MAKES ABOUT 2 DOZEN

Thumbprints bear the signatures of their bakers, who traditionally press their thumbs into the dough to form a well (but use a wooden spoon if you like). These buttery, crumbly shortbread cookies also have a signature pink lemon glaze, thanks to a single crushed raspberry. To make the cookies extra tender, we used confectioners' sugar instead of granulated sugar, and made the glaze from it as well.

2½ cups unbleached all-purpose flour

2 cups confectioners' sugar, sifted, plus more for dusting

1 teaspoon coarse salt

2 sticks (1 cup) unsalted butter, room temperature

2 tablespoons finely grated lemon zest, plus ¼ cup fresh lemon juice (from 2 to 3 lemons)

1 fresh raspberry

1. Preheat oven to 325°F. In a large bowl, whisk together flour, ½ cup sugar, and the salt. In another large bowl, using an electric mixer on medium, beat butter with ¼ cup sugar, the lemon zest, and 2 tablespoons lemon juice until pale and fluffy, about 3 minutes. Gradually add flour mixture and mix on low until just combined.

2. Using a cookie scoop or tablespoon, scoop dough and roll into 1-inch balls. Transfer to parchment-lined baking sheets, spacing each about 2 inches apart. Freeze until firm, about 10 minutes.

3. Bake cookies 10 minutes. Remove sheets one at a time, and press your thumb or the end of a wooden spoon handle into the center of each ball to indent. Rotate sheets and continue to bake until golden on bottoms, 16 to 18 minutes more. Transfer sheets to wire racks and let cool completely.

4. In a small bowl, whisk together remaining 1¼ cups sugar and 2 tablespoons lemon juice with raspberry, breaking up berry. Using a fine-mesh sieve, dust cookies with sugar. Spoon glaze into indents and let set, about 10 minutes. (Cookies can be stored in an airtight container at room temperature up to 1 week.)

Masala Chai Tea Cakes

MAKES ABOUT 3 DOZEN

In this remix of the Russian tea cake, we let you drink your tea and eat it, too. Adding the elements of a fine Indian masala chai—black tea and a mix of sweet and savory spices—to the classic little sugar-dusted snowball gives it delightful complexity. As in the preparation of any good masala chai, the choice and intensity of spices can be tailored to your personal taste.

2 cups unbleached all-purpose flour

1 cup almond flour

2 tablespoons best-quality black tea, such as Darjeeling, coarsely ground in a spice grinder or with a mortar and pestle

¾ teaspoon coarse salt

½ teaspoon freshly ground pepper

1 teaspoon ground cinnamon

¾ teaspoon ground ginger

½ teaspoon ground cardamom

Pinch of ground cloves

2 sticks (1 cup) unsalted butter, room temperature

½ cup confectioners' sugar, sifted, plus more for rolling

1 teaspoon vanilla extract

1. Preheat oven to 325°F. In a medium bowl, whisk together both flours, the tea, salt, pepper, cinnamon, ginger, cardamom, and cloves. In a large bowl, with an electric mixer on medium-high, beat butter and sugar until pale and fluffy, about 3 minutes. Beat in vanilla. Gradually add flour mixture and mix on low just until a dough forms (see Tip).

2. Scoop tablespoons of dough and roll into balls. Transfer to parchment-lined baking sheets, spacing balls about 1 inch apart.

3. Bake cookies, rotating sheets halfway through, until set and golden on bottoms, 15 to 18 minutes. Cool cookies on sheets for 5 minutes.

4. Place some confectioners' sugar in a small bowl. Roll cookies in sugar and transfer to wire racks; let cool completely. Generously coat cookies in more sugar before serving or storing. (Cookies can be stored in an airtight container at room temperature up to 2 weeks.)

TIP

You can make the dough ahead and refrigerate it for up to 3 days or keep it frozen up to 1 month.

PERFECTING
BISCOTTI

These Italian cookies are made without butter or oil and twice-baked to crisp perfection. They offer a wonderful palette for layering flavors and even more texture. In these three variations, we went for a balance of rich ingredients like rum, chocolate, raisins, and dates, with flashes of citrus, the heat of chiles, or the crunch of nuts to make each unique. Biscotti's roots are Italian, but a baker's invention results in a cookie of many cultures.

Rum Raisin Biscotti

MAKES ABOUT 40

1 cup raisins

⅓ cup dark rum

3 cups unbleached all-purpose flour

1 cup granulated sugar

2 teaspoons baking powder

½ teaspoon coarse salt

3 large eggs, lightly beaten

1 tablespoon vanilla extract

2 teaspoons finely grated orange zest

7½ ounces white chocolate, melted (see page 248)

Sanding sugar, for dusting

1. Preheat oven to 350°F. Combine raisins and rum. Microwave 2 minutes; let cool.

2. In a large bowl, whisk together flour, sugar, baking powder, and salt. Using an electric mixer on medium, beat in eggs and vanilla until combined. Add raisin-rum mixture and orange zest and beat until combined.

3. Divide dough in half and transfer to a parchment-lined baking sheet. Form each half into a 2½-inch-wide, ¾-inch-tall log. Bake, rotating sheet halfway through, until dough is firm but gives slightly when pressed, 20 to 25 minutes. Transfer sheet to a wire rack to cool, 20 minutes.

4. With a serrated knife, cut logs into ¼-inch slices on the diagonal and arrange, cut side down, on parchment-lined baking sheets. Bake, rotating sheets and flipping biscotti halfway through, until biscotti are crisp and golden, about 15 minutes. Transfer sheets to wire racks to cool.

5. Dip ends of biscotti in melted chocolate. Transfer to parchment-lined baking sheets and let set slightly, about 10 minutes. Sprinkle with sanding sugar. Refrigerate until set, about 10 minutes. (Store in an airtight container at room temperature, up to 2 days, or freeze, up to 3 months.)

Mexican Chocolate Biscotti

MAKES ABOUT 40

1½ cups unbleached all-purpose flour

¾ cup unsweetened Dutch-process cocoa powder

Pinch of cayenne pepper, plus more for dusting (optional)

1 teaspoon ground cinnamon

1 cup sugar

2 teaspoons baking powder

½ teaspoon coarse salt

3 large eggs, lightly beaten

1 tablespoon vanilla extract

3 ounces bittersweet chocolate, coarsely chopped

7½ ounces milk chocolate, melted (see page 248)

---

1. Preheat oven to 350°F. In a large bowl, whisk together flour, cocoa powder, cayenne, cinnamon, sugar, baking powder, and salt. Using an electric mixer on medium, beat in eggs and vanilla until combined. Add chopped chocolate and beat until combined.

2. Divide dough in half and transfer to a parchment-lined baking sheet. Form each half into a 2½-inch-wide, ¾-inch-tall log. Bake, rotating sheet halfway through, until dough is firm but gives slightly when pressed, 20 to 25 minutes. Transfer sheet to a wire rack to cool, 20 minutes.

3. With a serrated knife, cut logs into ¼-inch slices on the diagonal and arrange, cut side down, on parchment-lined baking sheets. Bake, rotating sheets and flipping biscotti halfway through, until biscotti are crisp, about 15 minutes. Transfer sheets to wire racks to cool.

4. Dip ends of biscotti in melted chocolate. Transfer to parchment-lined sheets and let set slightly, about 10 minutes. Sprinkle with cayenne, if desired. Refrigerate until set, about 10 minutes. (Store in an airtight container at room temperature, up to 2 days, or freeze, up to 3 months.)

Brown-Sugar and Date Biscotti

MAKES ABOUT 40

3 cups unbleached all-purpose flour

¾ cup packed dark brown sugar

2 teaspoons baking powder

½ teaspoon coarse salt

3 large eggs, lightly beaten

1 tablespoon vanilla extract

¾ cup chopped pitted dates

¾ cup chopped toasted pecans (see page 248)

7½ ounces dark chocolate, melted (see page 248)

Pistachios, chopped

1. Preheat oven to 350°F. In a large bowl, whisk together flour, sugar, baking powder, and salt. Using an electric mixer on medium, beat in eggs and vanilla until combined. Add dates and pecans, and beat until combined.

2. Divide dough in half and transfer to a parchment-lined baking sheet. Form each half into a 2½-inch-wide, ¾-inch-tall log. Bake, rotating sheet halfway through, until dough is firm but gives slightly when pressed, 20 to 25 minutes. Transfer sheet to a wire rack, 20 minutes to cool.

3. With a serrated knife, cut logs into ¼-inch slices on the diagonal and arrange, cut side down, on parchment-lined baking sheets. Bake, rotating sheets and flipping biscotti halfway through, until biscotti are crisp and golden, about 15 minutes. Transfer sheets to wire racks to cool.

4. Dip ends of biscotti in melted chocolate. Transfer to parchment-lined sheets and let set slightly, about 10 minutes. Sprinkle with chopped pistachios. Refrigerate until set, about 10 minutes. (Store in an airtight container at room temperature, up to 2 days, or freeze, up to 3 months.)

Tips for Biscotti

● Try not to bake on a humid day when biscotti (as well as many other cookies) spread more and are softer. If you have to, place the unbaked logs in the refrigerator for about 20 minutes before placing in the oven.

● The dough can be sticky, so lightly flour your hands or coat them with cooking spray before shaping it into logs. Making the logs as uniform as possible promotes even baking.

● To make slicing the biscotti easier, let them cool and harden for at least 10 minutes before slicing with a serrated knife. But don't cool too long (more than 20 minutes) or they will be more apt to crumble.

● If you have two wire racks, place them on the baking sheets and bake the "sliced" biscotti on top to allow air circulation. This will ensure the cookie has a nicely crisp top and bottom.

● Biscotti may be the ideal make-ahead cookie (and cookie to gift). Stored in an airtight container, many varieties last more than a week (and up to a month), and they hold up when sent by mail.

● Cool slices completely before storing. If they do get stored too early and soften, put them on a baking sheet in a 300°F oven for 10 to 15 minutes to crisp again.

3

SOME ASSEMBLY REQUIRED

The only thing that can possibly top a cookie
is one that's topped (say, with marshmallows and
chocolate like a s'more), or two cookies
wrapped around a luscious filling.
That's a sandwich we can believe in.

Brazilian Wedding Cookies

MAKES ABOUT 15

Bite-sized cookies sandwiched around a delectable fruit center, Brazilian *casadinhos* are often served at weddings to symbolize the sweet union of the married couple. The cookies are typically filled with dulce de leche or, as in this heart-shaped version, guava.

FOR THE COOKIES

1¼ cups unbleached all-purpose flour, plus more for dusting

¾ cup cornstarch

½ teaspoon coarse salt

1 stick (½ cup) unsalted butter

¾ cup superfine sugar

1 large egg, room temperature

2 teaspoons vanilla extract

1 teaspoon finely grated lemon zest

FOR THE FILLING

12 ounces guava paste, cut into small pieces

½ cup confectioners' sugar, sifted

¼ teaspoon pink powdered food coloring

1. Make the cookies: In a medium bowl, whisk together flour, cornstarch, and salt. In a large bowl, with an electric mixer on medium, beat butter and superfine sugar until pale and fluffy, about 2 minutes. Add egg, vanilla, and lemon zest, and beat until well combined. With mixer on low, gradually add flour mixture; mix until just combined. Divide dough in half, shape each half into a disk, and wrap in plastic. Refrigerate until firm, about 1 hour.

2. Preheat oven to 350°F. Working with one disk at a time, roll out dough ⅛ inch thick on a lightly floured surface. Using a 1¾-inch heart-shaped cutter, cut out cookies. Transfer to parchment-lined baking sheets, spacing 1 inch apart. Refrigerate 20 minutes.

3. Bake cookies, rotating sheets halfway through, until edges are just golden but still pale on top, 12 to 14 minutes. Let cool about 5 minutes. Transfer cookies to wire racks and let cool completely.

4. Make the filling: In a small saucepan over medium heat, combine guava paste with ⅓ cup water. Cook, stirring occasionally, until paste has melted completely and mixture is smooth. Remove from heat and let cool completely.

5. Transfer to a piping bag fitted with a ¼-inch round tip. Pipe 1 tablespoon filling onto half the cookies, then sandwich with remaining cookies. In a small bowl, mix confectioners' sugar and food coloring until well combined. Sift over cookies. (Unfilled cookies can be stored in an airtight container at room temperature up to 3 days; filling can be refrigerated, covered, up to 3 days.)

Tiramisu Cookies

MAKES 30

Tira me sù is Venetian dialect for "pick me up," which these mini sweets beg you to do. They're a new take on the mascarpone-rich layered dessert. A creamy, liqueur-spiked filling is sandwiched between cookies flavored with espresso and cocoa powder and brushed with melted chocolate.

5 large eggs, separated

1 cup granulated sugar

3 tablespoons instant espresso powder

½ cup cake flour (not self-rising)

¼ teaspoon coarse salt

Unsweetened Dutch-process cocoa powder, for dusting

¾ cup mascarpone cheese

¾ cup confectioners' sugar, sifted

3 tablespoons almond-flavored liqueur, such as amaretto

½ teaspoon vanilla extract

6 ounces semisweet chocolate, melted (see page 248)

1. Preheat oven to 350°F. In a large bowl, with an electric mixer on medium, beat egg yolks and ½ cup granulated sugar until pale and stiff, about 3 minutes. Add espresso powder and beat for 2 minutes. Add flour and beat until just combined. (Mixture will be very thick.)

2. In another large bowl, using clean, dry beaters and with mixer on medium, beat egg whites and salt until foamy. With mixer running, add remaining ½ cup granulated sugar in a slow stream, beating until stiff peaks form, about 5 minutes. Fold whites into yolk mixture in 3 additions until well combined.

3. Transfer batter to a pastry bag fitted with a ½-inch round tip (such as Ateco #806). Pipe batter onto parchment-lined baking sheets into 60 lines that are 2 inches long and 1 inch wide, spacing 1 inch apart. Using a fine-mesh sieve, dust with cocoa powder.

4. Bake, rotating sheets halfway through, until firm, 14 to 16 minutes. Transfer cookies on parchment to wire racks and let cool completely. (Cookies can be stored in an airtight container at room temperature for up to 3 days.)

5. Stir together mascarpone, confectioners' sugar, liqueur, and vanilla until well combined. Cover and refrigerate for at least 15 minutes and up to 3 days.

6. When ready to serve, brush the cookies' flat sides with melted chocolate. Refrigerate, flat side up, until chocolate is firm, about 10 minutes.

7. Spread a generous ½ teaspoon mascarpone filling over chocolate side of half the cookies. Sandwich with remaining cookies. Serve immediately. (Cookies are best eaten the day they are made.)

Pistachio and Apricot Rugelach

MAKES ABOUT 4 DOZEN

Simmered dried apricots with a hint of vanilla are a wonderful combination of tart and sweet. (We tested apricot jam in this filling, and it just wasn't the same.) The mixture is slathered on rounds of cream cheese dough, which is sliced into wedges and rolled into crescents before baking. The dough and filling can be made a couple of days in advance and refrigerated (the dough disks wrapped in plastic, the filling in an airtight container) to make assembly easier.

FOR THE DOUGH

2 sticks (1 cup) unsalted butter, room temperature

8 ounces cream cheese, room temperature

1/4 cup granulated sugar

1/4 teaspoon coarse salt

2 cups unbleached all-purpose flour, plus more for dusting

FOR THE FILLING

2 cups dried apricots

2/3 cup granulated sugar

1 teaspoon vanilla extract

Pinch of coarse salt

1 cup shelled pistachios, preferably Sicilian

1 large egg, lightly whisked

Sanding sugar, for sprinkling

1. Make the dough: In a large bowl, with an electric mixer on medium-high, beat butter with cream cheese, granulated sugar, and salt until fluffy, about 3 minutes. Add flour and beat on low until just combined. Divide dough into thirds and form into disks; wrap each in plastic and refrigerate until firm, at least 1 hour and up to 2 days.

2. Make the filling: In a saucepan, bring apricots, 1 1/3 cups water, the granulated sugar, vanilla, and salt to a boil. Reduce heat to low; simmer until apricots are tender and most of liquid has been absorbed,

12 to 14 minutes. Transfer to a food processor and pulse until smooth. Let cool completely. (You should have about 2 cups filling; if not, thin slightly with water.)

3. Meanwhile, finely grind pistachios in a food processor. On a lightly floured surface, roll out one disk of dough to a 10-inch circle, 1/8 inch thick. Spread evenly with 2/3 cup apricot mixture. Sprinkle with 1/4 cup ground pistachios. With a pizza wheel, cut circle into quarters, then cut each quarter in half, then in half again, so you have 16 wedges. Starting at outside edge of each wedge, roll up into a crescent shape. Arrange 1 inch apart on a parchment-lined baking sheet. Brush with beaten egg, and sprinkle with sanding sugar and 1 tablespoon ground pistachios. Repeat with remaining dough. Refrigerate until firm, about 30 minutes.

4. Preheat oven to 325°F. Bake rugelach, rotating sheets halfway through, until golden brown, 35 to 40 minutes. Transfer sheets to wire racks; let cool completely. (Rugelach can be stored in an airtight container at room temperature up to 3 days.)

Raspberry-Jam Ice Diamonds

MAKES ABOUT 80

Delicate ice crystals forming on winter windowpanes inspired these meltingly tender diamond-shaped confections that when arranged together can form a star or snowflake. You won't taste the cream cheese in the cookie, but it's the secret to a soft, buttery texture.

4 sticks (2 cups) unsalted butter, room temperature

8 ounces cream cheese, room temperature

½ teaspoon coarse salt

1 cup confectioners' sugar, sifted, plus more for dusting

4 cups unbleached all-purpose flour

1 teaspoon vanilla extract

1 cup raspberry preserves

1. In a large bowl, with an electric mixer on medium-high, beat butter, cream cheese, salt, and ¼ cup sugar until pale and fluffy, about 3 minutes. With mixer on low, beat in flour, 1 cup at a time, then vanilla, until combined.

2. Divide dough in half; shape each half into a flat rectangle and wrap in plastic wrap. Refrigerate until firm but still pliable, about 45 minutes. (Dough can be refrigerated up to 2 days.)

3. Dust 3 tablespoons sugar on a piece of parchment. Place one rectangle of dough on top and dust with 3 tablespoons sugar. Roll out to just under ¼ inch thick. Trim to a 12-by-16-inch rectangle and transfer on parchment to a baking sheet. Freeze until firm, about 30 minutes. Repeat with other rectangle of dough.

4. Preheat oven to 350°F. Slide one sheet of dough on parchment onto a work surface. Using an offset spatula, evenly spread with preserves. Invert remaining sheet of dough on top; remove parchment and let stand until soft enough to cut but still firm. Trim edges, then cut horizontally into strips the width of a ruler. Repeat with same-size strips on the diagonal to create diamonds.

5. Freeze diamonds until firm, about 10 minutes. Transfer to baking sheets lined with clean parchment, spacing 1 inch apart. Freeze again until firm, about 10 minutes. Bake cookies, rotating sheets halfway through, until golden, 20 to 23 minutes. Let cool on baking sheets 5 minutes, then dust with sugar. Let cool completely before removing from parchment with a spatula. Preserves may cause them to stick. (Cookies can be stored in an airtight container at room temperature up to 3 days.)

Chocolate Hazelnut–Crusted Sandwich Cookies

MAKES 3 DOZEN

If ever there were a pair of ingredients made for each other, it's chocolate and hazelnuts. This cookie unites them beautifully, with crisp chocolate wafers sandwiching a fluffy filling, then rolled in a fine coating of toasted hazelnuts for a crunchy finish.

FOR THE COOKIES

1¼ cups cake flour (not self-rising)

¾ cup unsweetened Dutch-process cocoa powder

½ teaspoon baking powder

¼ teaspoon coarse salt

5 tablespoons unsalted butter, melted and cooled

1 large egg

¾ cup packed light brown sugar

FOR THE FILLING

3 sticks (1½ cups) unsalted butter, room temperature

3 cups confectioners' sugar, sifted

¾ teaspoon vanilla extract

¼ teaspoon coarse salt

6 ounces bittersweet chocolate, melted (see page 248) and cooled

1 cup toasted skinned hazelnuts (see page 248), very finely chopped

1. Make the cookies: In a medium bowl, whisk together flour, cocoa powder, baking powder, and salt. In a large bowl, whisk together butter and egg. Add brown sugar and whisk to combine. Gradually add flour mixture and stir with a spatula until just combined. Transfer to a sheet of plastic wrap.

2. Divide dough into thirds; roll out each third on a nonstick baking mat, topped with plastic wrap, to a $1/16$-inch thickness. Stack on a baking sheet and refrigerate until firm, about 30 minutes.

3. Preheat oven to 350°F. Using a 2-inch cookie cutter, cut dough into rounds, then transfer rounds to parchment-lined baking sheets. Reroll scraps one time to make a total of 72 cookies. (If dough becomes soft, place in freezer until firm.) Bake cookies, rotating sheets halfway through, until firm and fragrant, 9 to 10 minutes. Transfer sheets to wire racks and let cool.

4. Make the filling: In a large bowl, with an electric mixer on low, beat butter, confectioners' sugar, vanilla, and salt. Begin beating on low, then increase to high for 2 minutes, scraping down the sides of the bowl occasionally. Stir in melted chocolate to combine.

5. Spread 2 tablespoons filling on half the cookies, then sandwich with remaining cookies. Roll edges in chopped hazelnuts to adhere. Chill overnight before serving. (Assembled cookies can be refrigerated in an airtight container up to 2 days.)

S'mores Cookies

You don't have to be gathered around a campfire to enjoy a chocolatey, gooey, marshmallowy s'more. Here, an oatmeal cookie substitutes for the standard graham-cracker base, your broiler for the campfire. Just leave them under the flame a touch longer if you like your marshmallows a little more toasted.

½ cup old-fashioned rolled oats

1 cup unbleached all-purpose flour

1 cup whole-wheat flour

¾ teaspoon ground cinnamon

½ teaspoon baking soda

½ teaspoon coarse salt

2 sticks (1 cup) unsalted butter, room temperature

¾ cup packed light brown sugar

1 large egg, room temperature

8 ounces bittersweet or semisweet chocolate, cut into 30 squares

15 large marshmallows, halved horizontally

1. Preheat oven to 350°F. In a food processor, pulse oats until finely ground. Add both flours, cinnamon, baking soda, and salt; pulse to combine.

2. In a large bowl, using an electric mixer on medium, beat butter and sugar until pale and fluffy, about 3 minutes. Beat in egg, scraping down sides of bowl. With mixer on low, beat in flour mixture until combined.

3. Using a cookie scoop or a tablespoon, drop dough by tablespoons onto parchment-lined baking sheets, spacing 1 inch apart. Top each with a chocolate square. Bake cookies, rotating sheets halfway through, just until lightly golden, 11 to 13 minutes. Remove sheets from oven; heat broiler. Top each cookie with a marshmallow half. One sheet at a time, broil until marshmallows are lightly browned, 1 to 1½ minutes. Transfer cookies to wire racks to cool. (Cookies are best eaten the day they are made.)

TIP

For added texture and a nutty sweetness, substitute regular whole-wheat flour with graham flour, a very coarsely stone-ground whole-wheat flour that's used in graham crackers.

Chocolate Malt Sandwich Cookies

MAKES 54

Chocolate meets chocolate for a truly decadent treat—the ideal accompaniment to an afternoon coffee or espresso. Wafer-thin cookies with a hint of malted flavor sandwich a salted ganache that is rich, buttery, and smooth. When making the filling, bring the cream just to a boil and then pour it over the chocolate with a sprinkle of salt.

FOR THE COOKIES

2 cups plus
2 tablespoons
all-purpose flour

½ cup unsweetened
natural cocoa powder

¼ cup plain
malted-milk powder

1 teaspoon
baking soda

½ teaspoon
coarse salt

2 sticks (1 cup)
unsalted butter,
room temperature

1¾ cups sugar

1 large egg

2 teaspoons
vanilla extract

¼ cup crème fraîche

3 tablespoons
hot water

FOR THE FILLING

20 ounces milk
chocolate, coarsely
chopped

1¼ cups heavy cream

1¼ teaspoons
coarse salt

1. **Make cookies:** Preheat oven to 350°F. Whisk together flour, cocoa powder, malt powder, baking soda, and salt into a medium bowl.

2. In a medium bowl, with an electric mixer on medium, beat butter and sugar until pale and fluffy, about 4 minutes. Add egg and vanilla, and beat until combined. Mix in crème fraîche. Mix in hot water. With mixer on low, gradually add flour mixture and beat until just incorporated.

3. Using a ½-ounce cookie scoop, drop dough onto parchment-lined baking sheets, spacing about 2 inches apart (or use a tablespoon; gently shape dough into balls). Bake cookies, rotating sheets halfway through, until tops flatten and cookies are just firm, 10 to 12 minutes. Transfer to wire racks and let cool completely.

4. **Make the filling:** Place chocolate in a medium bowl. In a small saucepan, bring cream just to a boil over medium-high heat. Pour over chocolate and add salt. Let stand for 10 minutes (do not stir—doing so will cool the ganache too quickly, making it grainy). Using a whisk, stir ganache until smooth and shiny, scraping down sides of bowl as needed.

5. **Assemble the cookies:** Spread 1 table-spoon of filling on a cookie with an offset spatula. Sandwich with a second cookie. Repeat with remaining cookies. (Cookies can be refrigerated in an airtight container up to 2 days.)

Lime Sandwich Cookies

MAKES 30

For this two-bite take on Brazilian limonada (a frothy, refreshing drink made with limes and condensed milk), swirl a dollop of tangy citrus filling between two sugar cookies. Use a teardrop aspic cutter to give some of the cookies a citrus-slice look before baking—or simply sift confectioners' sugar over the tops for a photo-worthy finish.

3 cups unbleached all-purpose flour, plus more for dusting

¼ teaspoon baking powder

Coarse salt

2 sticks (1 cup) plus 6 tablespoons unsalted butter, room temperature

1¾ cups confectioners' sugar, sifted

1 large egg, room temperature

1 teaspoon vanilla extract

12 ounces (1 cup) sweetened condensed milk

1 teaspoon grated zest plus 6 tablespoons fresh lime juice (6 to 8 limes)

3 ounces cream cheese, room temperature

1. In a large bowl, whisk together flour, baking powder, and 1 teaspoon salt. In another bowl, with an electric mixer on high, beat 2 sticks butter with sugar until pale and fluffy, about 4 minutes. Beat in egg, vanilla, and 1 tablespoon water. With mixer on low, add flour mixture and beat until just combined. Divide dough in half and shape into disks. Wrap in plastic and freeze until firm, about 30 minutes.

2. Preheat oven to 325°F. Remove one disk from freezer; let stand at room temperature 15 minutes. On a lightly floured surface, roll out dough ⅛ inch thick. Using a 2½-inch cutter, stamp out rounds. Transfer rounds to parchment-lined baking sheets, spacing about 1 inch apart. Roll scraps; cut out more rounds. Repeat with other disk for a total of 60 rounds. With a teardrop aspic cutter, cut ¾-inch teardrops from half of rounds. Refrigerate 30 minutes. Bake cookies, rotating sheets halfway through, until edges are golden, about 20 minutes. Transfer sheets to wire racks and let cool completely.

3. In a small pan over medium-high, heat condensed milk, stirring frequently, until bubbling. Reduce heat to medium and continue to cook, stirring, until it reaches the consistency of pudding, about 5 minutes. Strain through a fine-mesh sieve into a bowl. Whisk in lime zest and juice and a pinch of salt. Cover surface directly with plastic and refrigerate 30 minutes.

4. In a medium bowl, with an electric mixer on medium-high, beat remaining 6 tablespoons butter, the cream cheese, and milk mixture until fluffy. Spread 2 teaspoons filling on a solid cookie; top with a cutout. Repeat with remaining cookies. Refrigerate, covered, at least 1 hour before serving. (Cookies can be refrigerated in an airtight container up to 4 days.)

Peanut-Butter Sandwich Cookies

MAKES 1 DOZEN

Oaty and nutty, this sandwich cookie will delight peanut butter and oatmeal cookie lovers alike. Toasted oats give the cookies crunch—the better to envelop a smooth, creamy peanut-butter filling.

FOR THE COOKIES

1½ sticks (¾ cup) unsalted butter, room temperature

1 cup old-fashioned rolled oats

1 cup plus 2 tablespoons unbleached all-purpose flour

1 teaspoon baking soda

1 teaspoon coarse salt

½ cup packed dark brown sugar

⅓ cup granulated sugar

½ cup smooth peanut butter

Turbinado sugar, for sprinkling

FOR THE FILLING

4 tablespoons unsalted butter, room temperature

¾ cup smooth peanut butter

¼ cup confectioners' sugar, sifted

½ teaspoon coarse salt

1. Make the cookies: In a medium saucepan over medium heat, melt ½ stick (4 tablespoons) butter. Add oats and cook, stirring, until toasted, 5 to 10 minutes. Spread oat mixture onto a parchment-lined baking sheet and let cool.

2. In a medium bowl, whisk together flour, baking soda, and salt. In a large bowl, with an electric mixer on medium-high, beat remaining 1 stick butter, and brown and granulated sugars until pale and fluffy, about 3 minutes. Add peanut butter and mix until well combined.

3. Gradually add oat mixture and flour mixture, and mix on low until combined. Roll out dough between 2 sheets of parchment to ¼ inch thick. Slide dough with parchment onto baking sheet and refrigerate until chilled, about 20 minutes.

4. Preheat oven to 350°F. Remove top layer of parchment; cut out cookies using a 2-inch round cookie cutter. Place cookies on parchment-lined baking sheets, spacing about 1 inch apart; sprinkle with turbinado sugar. Bake until golden, about 10 minutes. Let cool completely on baking sheets.

5. Make the filling: In a medium bowl, with an electric mixer on medium, mix all ingredients until smooth. Transfer filling to a pastry bag fitted with a ½-inch round tip (such as Ateco #806).

6. Pipe filling in a spiral motion on bottom side of half the cookies (see page 242 for how to pipe filling). Top with remaining cookies to form sandwiches. (Filled cookies can be stored in an airtight container at room temperature up to 3 days.)

Passionfruit Melting Moments

MAKES 2 DOZEN

One bite and you'll know how these cookies got their name. They literally melt in your mouth. Found at cafés all over Australia and New Zealand, melting moments are also known as cornstarch cookies, or, when filled, as custard kisses. Fillings can be made in a variety of flavors, from vanilla to raspberry— Martha chose homemade passionfruit curd for these.

FOR THE COOKIES

1½ sticks (¾ cup) unsalted butter, room temperature

½ cup confectioners' sugar, sifted, plus more for dusting

1 tablespoon vanilla extract

1¼ cups unbleached all-purpose flour

¼ cup cornstarch

½ teaspoon coarse salt

FOR THE FILLING

4 large egg yolks

½ cup frozen passionfruit puree, defrosted

½ cup granulated sugar

½ teaspoon coarse salt

5 tablespoons cold unsalted butter

1 teaspoon unflavored gelatin

1. Make the cookies: In a large bowl, with an electric mixer on medium-high, beat butter, confectioners' sugar, and vanilla, scraping down sides as necessary, until pale and fluffy, about 2 minutes. In a medium bowl, sift together flour and cornstarch. Add flour mixture to butter mixture along with salt, beating until just combined. Cover with plastic wrap and refrigerate 1 hour.

2. Preheat oven to 350°F. Scoop 2 teaspoons of dough at a time and roll into 48 balls; transfer to parchment-lined baking sheet, spacing about 1 inch apart. Use a fork to make long indents on tops of balls. Bake cookies until slightly golden around edges, 10 to 12 minutes. Transfer baking sheets to wire racks and let cool completely.

3. Make the filling: In a medium saucepan over medium heat, combine egg yolks, passionfruit puree, granulated sugar, and salt. Cook, stirring constantly, until mixture is thick enough to coat the back of a spoon, about 10 minutes. Stir in butter and gelatin, mixing until the butter has melted and the gelatin has dissolved. Using a fine-mesh sieve, strain curd into a medium bowl, then place plastic wrap directly onto surface; refrigerate until set, at least 1 hour.

4. Spread 1 scant teaspoon curd on flat side of half the cookies. Dust remaining cookies with confectioners' sugar; sandwich halves together. (Filled cookies are best eaten the day they are made; unfilled cookies can be stored in an airtight container at room temperature up to 2 weeks.)

Macaroon Sandwich Cookies

MAKES ABOUT 45

Macaroon, meet macaron. Lending a French accent to the traditional Passover treat—by sandwiching preserves between two of the crisp, chewy coconut cookies—you get a simply unique dessert. Just about any jam complements the macaroon's flaky layers. For these, we used mango, raspberry, and apricot for a variety of color and flavor.

2 large egg whites

3 tablespoons sugar

Pinch of coarse salt

8 ounces sweetened flaked coconut

½ cup jam, such as mango, raspberry, or apricot

1. Preheat oven to 350°F. In a medium bowl, whisk together egg whites, sugar, and salt until frothy. Stir in coconut until moist. Drop teaspoon-size mounds onto parchment-lined baking sheets; flatten with a fork. Bake cookies, rotating sheets halfway through, until golden, 13 to 15 minutes. Let cool completely.

2. Spread ½ teaspoon jam on flat side of half the cookies, then sandwich with remaining cookies. (Cookies can be stored in an airtight container at room temperature up to 3 days.)

TIP

This cookie calls for sweetened coconut, in which sugar is added before the coconut is dried, versus unsweetened coconut, which is simply dried. The sweetened version tends to be more moist, with a bolder flavor.

Maple-Cream Sandwich Cookies

MAKES ABOUT 20

Maple infuses all the layers of these leaf-shaped sandwich cookies: Maple sugar goes into the buttery shortbread dough and maple syrup sweetens the cream filling. Golden or amber maple syrups are what most cooks use, but if you like a stronger maple flavor, go for the darker syrups, which are produced later in the season.

FOR THE COOKIES

5 cups unbleached all-purpose flour, plus more for dusting

1 tablespoon plus 1 teaspoon baking powder

2 teaspoons ground cinnamon

½ teaspoon coarse salt

4 sticks (2 cups) unsalted butter, room temperature

2 cups granulated sugar

1 cup pure maple sugar

2 large eggs, room temperature

FOR THE FILLING

1½ sticks (¾ cup) unsalted butter, room temperature

3 cups confectioners' sugar, sifted

6 tablespoons pure maple syrup

1. Make the cookies: In a large bowl, whisk together flour, baking powder, cinnamon, and salt. In another bowl, with an electric mixer on medium, beat butter and granulated and maple sugars until pale and fluffy, about 3 minutes. Add eggs and beat until combined, about 30 seconds. Add flour mixture and mix on low until just combined, about 30 seconds, scraping down sides as necessary. Divide dough into 4 pieces, shape into disks, and wrap each in plastic. Refrigerate at least 1 hour.

2. Preheat oven to 375°F. On a lightly floured surface, roll out one disk of dough to ⅛-inch thickness, lightly dusting with flour. Cut out about 10 cookies using a 4-inch maple-leaf–shaped cutter, dipping cutter in flour as needed. Transfer to parchment-lined baking sheets and freeze until firm, about 10 minutes. Repeat process with remaining disks of dough.

3. Bake cookies, rotating sheets halfway through, until edges begin to brown, 10 to 12 minutes. Transfer sheets to wire racks and let cool. Transfer cookies to wire racks and let cool completely.

4. Make the filling: In a medium bowl, with an electric mixer on medium-high, beat butter until pale and fluffy, about 2 minutes. Add confectioners' sugar and maple syrup; beat until smooth. Transfer to a pastry bag fitted with a small round tip (such as Ateco #1 or #2). Pipe 2 tablespoons filling onto bottoms of half the cookies, then sandwich with remaining cookies. (Filled cookies can be stored in an airtight container at room temperature up to 3 days.)

Pumpkin-Gingerbread Ice Cream Sandwiches

MAKES 15

Pumpkin pairs naturally with warm spices such as ground ginger, cinnamon, and nutmeg. So it's no surprise that here we combine pumpkin ice cream with chewy gingerbread cookies; but feel free to use your favorite vanilla if you prefer. Whichever flavor you choose, soften it in the refrigerator for 30 minutes before scooping to make the ice cream sandwiches.

3 cups plus 2 tablespoons unbleached all-purpose flour

2 tablespoons unsweetened Dutch-process cocoa powder

2½ teaspoons ground ginger

2 teaspoons ground cinnamon

½ teaspoon ground cloves

¼ teaspoon freshly grated nutmeg

2 sticks (1 cup) unsalted butter, room temperature

1 cup packed dark brown sugar

2 tablespoons finely grated peeled fresh ginger

½ cup unsulfured molasses

⅓ cup granulated sugar

Store-bought pumpkin or vanilla ice cream

1. In a medium bowl, sift together flour, cocoa powder, ginger, cinnamon, cloves, and nutmeg. In a large bowl, with an electric mixer on medium, beat butter, brown sugar, and grated ginger until fluffy, about 3 minutes. Beat in molasses. Gradually add flour mixture and mix on low until combined. Form dough into a disk and wrap in plastic. Refrigerate until firm, about 2 hours and up to overnight.

2. Scoop dough into thirty 1½-inch balls and transfer to parchment-lined baking sheets, spacing about 2 inches apart. Refrigerate 20 minutes.

3. Preheat oven to 325°F. Roll balls in granulated sugar. Bake until surfaces crack slightly, 10 to 12 minutes. Let cool about 5 minutes. Transfer cookies to wire racks and let cool completely.

4. Place 15 cookies, flat sides up, on a baking sheet. Scoop ⅓ cup ice cream into center of each cookie. Place remaining cookies, flat side down, on top of ice cream. Gently press with flattened palm until ice cream spreads to edges of cookies. Freeze until ice cream is semi-firm, about 2 hours. (Sandwiches can be frozen on baking sheet until firm, about 4 hours more, and then stored in a freezer bag up to 2 weeks.) To serve, transfer cookies to refrigerator until ice cream softens slightly, about 30 minutes.

PERFECTING
FRENCH MACARONS

Turn your kitchen into a *pâtisserie* by creating light-as-air macarons at home. Because precision matters with these confections, we recommend weighing the ingredients and following the tips for making the meringue. As for flavors, we offer five variations. Whether you prepare just one or mix and match, you'll have professional-looking (and -tasting) results that will have people wondering which fancy French bakery you bought them from.

MAKES 20 TO 25

²/₃ cup sliced blanched almonds (71 grams)

1 cup confectioners' sugar (117 grams), sifted

2 large egg whites, room temperature

¼ cup granulated sugar (53 grams)

Flavoring and food coloring (see page 112)

Filling (see page 112)

---

1. Preheat oven to 350°F. In a food processor, process almonds as finely as possible, about 1 minute. Add confectioners' sugar and process until combined, about 1 minute.

2. Pass mixture through a fine-mesh sieve. Transfer solids in sieve to food processor, and then grind and sift again, pressing down on clumps. Repeat until less than 2 tablespoons of solids remain in sieve.

3. In a large bowl, whisk egg whites and granulated sugar by hand to combine. With an electric mixer on medium, beat 2 minutes. With mixer on high, beat 2 minutes more, until stiff, glossy peaks form. Add flavoring and food coloring, if desired, and beat on high for 30 seconds.

4. Gradually add dry ingredients. Fold with a spatula from bottom of bowl upward (see A, page 113), then press flat side of spatula firmly through middle of mixture (see B). Repeat just until batter flows like lava, 35 to 40 complete strokes.

5. Transfer batter to a pastry bag fitted with a ⅜-inch round tip (Ateco #804; see C). Dab some batter onto corners of 2 baking sheets; line with parchment.

6. With piping tip ½ inch above sheet, pipe batter into a ¾-inch round, then swirl tip off to one side (see D). Repeat, spacing rounds 1 inch apart. Tap sheets against counter 2 or 3 times to release air bubbles.

7. Bake one sheet at a time, until cookies have risen and just set, about 13 minutes, rotating halfway through. Let cool completely. Pipe or spread filling on flat sides of half the cookies; top with remaining half. Wrap in plastic and refrigerate. (Macarons are best eaten after 1 or more days of refrigeration.)

Mix-and-Match Flavors and Fillings

Think of the basic almond cookie as the starting point for countless adaptations. Here are five of our favorites. You can modify the hue and flavor (in step 3) as desired.

1. Espresso

Cookie: Add ½ teaspoon instant espresso powder. Sift more powder over half the unbaked rounds. (Mocha variation: Replace ⅓ cup confectioners' sugar with ¼ cup unsweetened cocoa powder.) **Filling:** Dissolve ¼ teaspoon instant espresso powder in ¼ teaspoon hot water; mix into ⅔ cup Swiss meringue buttercream (see page 246). **Best eaten:** After 3 to 5 days of refrigeration.

2. Rose Raspberry

Cookie: Add ¼ teaspoon rose water and 3 drops rose-pink gel-paste food coloring. **Filling:** ½ cup raspberry jam (with seeds). **Best eaten:** After 1 to 2 days of refrigeration.

3. Toasted Hazelnut and Chocolate

Cookie: Substitute toasted skinned hazelnuts for almonds. **Filling:** Heat ¼ cup heavy cream in a saucepan until bubbles begin to form. Add 1½ ounces finely chopped bittersweet chocolate and ½ tablespoon unsalted butter; stir to combine. Stir in 3 tablespoons chocolate-hazelnut spread. Let cool until thick and spreadable. **Best eaten:** After 1 to 2 days of refrigeration.

4. Chocolate Mint

Cookie: Add ¼ teaspoon peppermint extract and 2 drops leaf-green gel-paste food coloring. Finely grate bittersweet chocolate over half the unbaked rounds. **Filling:** Heat ¼ cup heavy cream in a saucepan until bubbles begin to form. Add 1½ ounces finely chopped bittersweet chocolate and ½ tablespoon unsalted butter; stir to combine. Let cool until thick and spreadable. **Best eaten:** After 1 to 2 days of refrigeration.

5. Vanilla Bean

Cookie: Add seeds from ½ vanilla bean and 1 drop copper gel-paste food coloring. **Filling:** ⅔ cup Swiss meringue buttercream (see page 246). **Best eaten:** After 3 to 5 days of refrigeration.

Tips for Macarons

- Fresh egg whites are the key to meringue that rises well in the oven. Older whites may collapse. Don't use packaged egg whites—the pasteurization process can prevent them from forming a stable meringue.

- To avoid a granular texture, add the almond-sugar mixture to the foam gradually, and be careful not to overbeat the mixture. The meringue should be smooth, glossy, and flexible, not dry or grainy.

- If using food coloring in the batter, use gel, not liquid. Liquid coloring can make your batter runny.

- To avoid cracks in the meringue, open the oven door as little as possible. If the meringue is starting to brown at all, reduce the oven temperature by 25 degrees.

- Piping the perfect macaron takes a little practice. Treat it as you would a rosette, bringing the pastry tip to the side of the circle, rather than forming a peak, to finish. You can also use a macaron baking mat marked with circles to guide you.

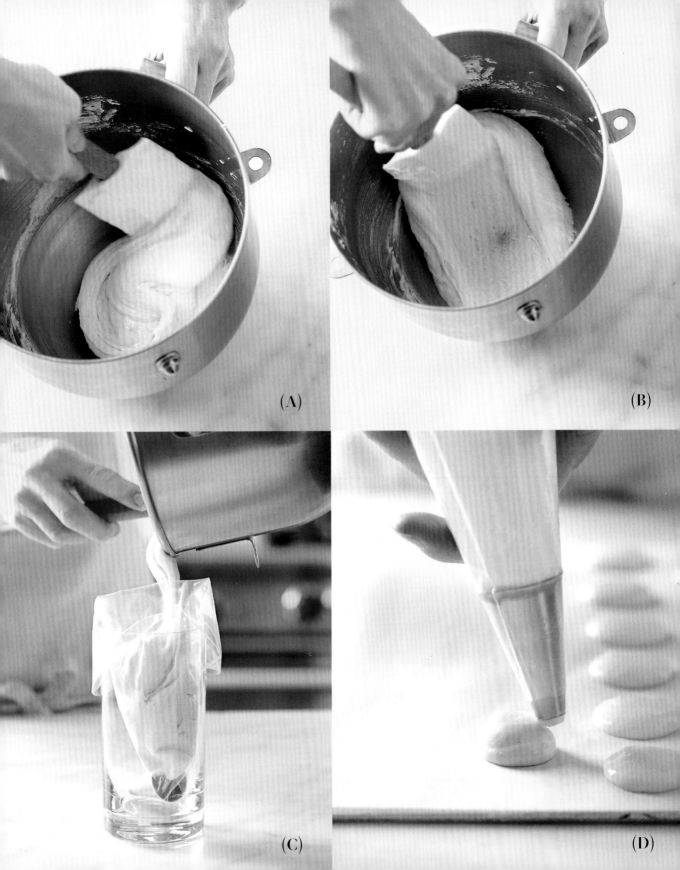

(A)

(B)

(C)

(D)

4
GIANT COOKIES

A big cookie for a big sweet tooth, or for sharing with a big group of friends, or for a hearty breakfast. Whatever the reason to go big, supersizing is simply big fun.

PERFECTING
SUGAR COOKIES

Classic sugar cookies take baking back to basics. But in their simplicity lies their perfection: It's hard to beat the delicate flavor of cookies with only the most elemental of ingredients. Here, we veered from tradition in just a few details: We added sour cream to make them extra soft, and we made them giant because that's how much we adore them. Lemon glaze and candied citrus zest offer a bit of adornment, while homemade sprinkles supply some old-fashioned charm.

MAKES 10

2 cups unbleached all-purpose flour

1 teaspoon baking powder

½ teaspoon coarse salt

¼ teaspoon baking soda

1 stick (½ cup) unsalted butter, room temperature

1½ cups sugar, plus more for sprinkling

1 large egg

1 teaspoon vanilla extract

¼ cup sour cream

1. Preheat oven to 350°F. In a medium bowl, whisk together flour, baking powder, salt, and baking soda. In a large bowl, with an electric mixer on medium-high, beat butter and sugar until pale and fluffy, about 3 minutes. Add egg and vanilla, and beat well to combine.

2. With mixer on low, add half the flour mixture, followed by sour cream, then remaining flour mixture; mix just until smooth. (Dough will be stiff; you may need to finish mixing it with a wooden spoon.)

3. Using a cookie scoop or a tablespoon, scoop dough (3 tablespoons) and drop on parchment-lined baking sheets, spacing 3 to 4 inches apart.

4. Bake, rotating sheets halfway through, until edges of cookies are just firm and tops are barely beginning to brown, 20 to 25 minutes. Transfer cookies to wire racks and let cool completely. (Cookies can be stored in an airtight container at room temperature for 5 days.)

VARIATIONS

Glazed with Citrus

Dip cooled cookies in Lemon Glaze (page 246), letting excess drip back into bowl, at end of step 4. Transfer to a wire rack and immediately decorate with candied citrus (see page 248); let set.

With Sprinkles

At end of Step 2, stir in about half of the Homemade Sprinkles. At end of Step 3, pat remaining Homemade Sprinkles around scooped dough.

Homemade Sprinkles

MAKES 1¼ CUPS

1½ cups confectioners' sugar, sifted
1 tablespoon light corn syrup
¼ teaspoon vanilla extract
Pink, peach, and fuchsia gel-paste food coloring

---

1. Combine sugar, 2 tablespoons water, corn syrup, and vanilla in a small bowl. Stir until mixture has consistency of glue, adding more water if necessary, ¼ teaspoon at a time. Divide into 3 small bowls; tint with food coloring until desired color is achieved.

2. Transfer lightest-colored mixture to a pastry bag fitted with a small round tip (such as Ateco #2). Pipe long, thin lines onto parchment-lined baking sheets. Repeat with medium-colored mixture, then with darkest-colored mixture. Let stand, uncovered, until very firm, at least overnight. Once lines are dry, break or cut into small pieces.

Tips for Sugar Cookies

● Try different flavorings for the dough: freshly grated zest from half a lemon or a tablespoon of cognac. Add in step 1, right after the vanilla.

● When you're making the candied orange and lemon zest, leave most of the fruit's pith on the citrus peel. It adds heft, not bitterness as it does when uncooked.

● To give plain sugar cookies a delicate crust, sprinkle scooped cookie dough with a double layer of sanding or granulated sugar. Sprinkle dough once, then lightly brush with a pastry brush moistened in cool water, then sprinkle with more sanding sugar. Refrigerate before baking.

● Store-bought sprinkles can leave a waxy taste in your mouth. But homemade sprinkles just taste like sugar and vanilla. The extras will keep in an airtight container at room temperature up to a month.

● For the homemade sprinkles, when tinting with food coloring, try dipping a toothpick into the food coloring and adding to the sugar mixture. Adding color a little at a time this way helps you better control the desired shade.

● If you prefer soft cookies, slightly underbake them. They should be golden around the edges but can remain pale in the center.

● These are technically "old-fashioned," as they are drop cookies. As with any drop cookie with a high sugar content, if your cookies come out slightly misshapen, take a small offset spatula and shape the edges. Do this as soon as the cookies come out of the oven, as they're more malleable when hot.

● Give sugar cookies enough time to cool on wire racks before moving them—they need to firm up a bit first.

Kitchen-Sink Cookies

MAKES 8

Tart dried fruit, toasted nuts, chocolate, rolled oats, even coconut flakes (which are slightly thicker and more "meaty" than shredded coconut)— everything but the kitchen sink is included in this recipe. If you're making a cookie this good, think big. Really big.

2 sticks (1 cup) unsalted butter, room temperature

¾ cup granulated sugar

¾ cup packed light brown sugar

2 large eggs

2 teaspoons vanilla extract

2 cups unbleached all-purpose flour

1 teaspoon coarse salt

1 teaspoon baking soda

½ teaspoon baking powder

1½ cups old-fashioned rolled oats

1 cup large unsweetened coconut flakes

1 cup dried apricots, coarsely chopped

6 ounces semi-sweet chocolate, coarsely chopped

1 cup dried cherries

1 cup pecans, toasted (see page 248)

1. Preheat oven to 350°F. In a large bowl, with an electric mixer on medium, beat butter and both sugars until pale and fluffy, about 2 minutes. With mixer on low, beat in eggs, one at a time, until combined. Beat in vanilla.

2. In a medium bowl, whisk together flour, salt, baking soda, and baking powder. With mixer on low, gradually add to butter mixture, beating until well combined.

Add oats, coconut, apricots, chocolate, cherries, and pecans, and mix with a wooden spoon until just combined.

3. Scoop dough into 8 balls (¾ cup each). Transfer to parchment-lined baking sheets, spacing about 3 inches apart. Use the palm of your hand to flatten into 4-inch rounds. Bake cookies, rotating sheets halfway through, until golden brown, about 16 minutes. Let cookies cool on sheet 2 minutes before transferring to wire racks to cool completely. (Cookies can be stored in an airtight container at room temperature up to 3 days.)

TIP

Feel free to customize the add-ins: If you don't like pecans, use walnuts; try cranberries instead of cherries. Just make sure there's enough space between the cookies, as they spread in the oven.

Chocolate–Chocolate Chip Skillet Cookie

MAKES 12 SERVINGS

Baking doesn't get any easier than this big cookie with the double hit of fudgy flavor. All the ingredients can be stirred in a single bowl, and there's no scooping and portioning the dough. Just mix, pour into a nonstick skillet, bake, and slice. The wedges are especially delicious warm, topped with a scoop of vanilla ice cream.

6 tablespoons unsalted butter, room temperature

¾ cup packed light brown sugar

1 large egg, room temperature

1 teaspoon vanilla extract

1 cup unbleached all-purpose flour

2 tablespoons unsweetened Dutch-process cocoa powder

½ teaspoon baking soda

½ teaspoon coarse salt

1½ cups (10 ounces) semisweet chocolate chips

1. Preheat oven to 350°F. In a large bowl, mix butter and sugar with a wooden spoon until combined. Stir in egg and vanilla; then flour, cocoa powder, baking soda, and salt. Stir in chocolate chips.

2. Transfer batter to a 10-inch ovenproof nonstick skillet and smooth top with an offset spatula. Bake, rotating halfway through, until just set in center and pulling away from sides, 20 to 22 minutes. Let cool, about 10 minutes, before slicing and serving.

TIP

For a chocolate-chip topping, reserve ¼ cup chocolate chips for sprinkling on top before baking.

"Jamaretti" Cookies

MAKES 4 LARGE COOKIES/ABOUT 3 DOZEN SERVINGS

Think of these sliced, almond-flavored, jam-filled cookies as a super-sized hybrid of biscotti and thumbprints. Here, instead of pressing the center of each round of dough, as you would a typical thumbprint, the dough remains in logs. You use the handle of a wooden spoon to form a trench to fill with jam, then bake and slice them like you would biscotti.

2¼ cups unbleached all-purpose flour, plus more for dusting

1 teaspoon baking powder

1 teaspoon coarse salt

½ teaspoon ground cinnamon

½ cup almond paste

¾ cup granulated sugar

1 stick (½ cup) unsalted butter, room temperature

2 large eggs, room temperature

½ cup jam (blackberry, raspberry, or apricot)

1 cup confectioners' sugar, sifted

4 teaspoons whole milk

1. In a large bowl, whisk together flour, baking powder, salt, and cinnamon. In a food processor, pulse almond paste and granulated sugar until smooth. Add butter and eggs to sugar mixture, and blend until smooth. Add flour mixture and pulse until dough forms. Divide into 4 equal pieces, wrap in plastic, and chill 30 minutes. (At this point, dough can be frozen up to 1 week; just thaw it in the refrigerator overnight before using.)

2. Preheat oven to 350°F. On a lightly floured surface, roll each piece into a 10-inch log. Transfer logs to 2 parchment-lined baking sheets and flatten to about 2 inches across. Bake until just dry, 12 to 15 minutes.

3. Using the handle of a wooden spoon, make a trench down center of each log. Spread 2 tablespoons jam into each trench. Return to oven and bake until golden brown, 8 to 10 minutes more. Transfer sheets to wire racks and let cool completely.

4. In a small bowl, whisk together the confectioners' sugar and milk until smooth. Drizzle glaze over logs. Let glaze harden, about 20 minutes. With a serrated knife, cut logs on the diagonal into 1-inch slices. (Cookies can be stored in an airtight container at room temperature up to 3 days.)

Mighty Australian Ginger Cookies

MAKES 1 DOZEN

Ginger lovers can unite over what Australians call ginger nuts, a favorite cookie Down Under. There are no nuts in the recipe, though our version goes a little nutty over the main ingredient, calling for ginger three ways—dried, fresh, and crystallized.

2½ cups unbleached all-purpose flour

2 teaspoons ground ginger

1 teaspoon freshly ground pepper

1 teaspoon freshly grated nutmeg

1 teaspoon baking soda

½ teaspoon coarse salt

1 stick (½ cup) unsalted butter, room temperature

1 cup packed light brown sugar

½ cup granulated sugar

1 tablespoon grated peeled fresh ginger

2 large eggs, room temperature

¼ cup golden syrup

¼ cup chopped crystallized ginger

¼ cup fine sanding sugar

1. In a large bowl, whisk together flour, ground ginger, pepper, nutmeg, baking soda, and salt. In another large bowl, with an electric mixer on medium, beat butter, brown and granulated sugars, and grated ginger until pale and fluffy, about 2 minutes. Add eggs, one at a time, beating well after each addition. Add golden syrup and continue to beat, scraping down sides as necessary, until thoroughly combined. Mix in crystallized ginger. With mixer on low, gradually add flour mixture and mix until just combined. Cover with plastic wrap and refrigerate until firm, at least 2 hours.

2. Using a ¼-cup ice cream scoop, drop dough onto a parchment-lined baking sheet. (If dough becomes soft, refrigerate 20 minutes.) Roll dough into balls between your palms, then roll in sanding sugar to coat. Transfer to parchment-lined baking sheets, spacing about 2 inches apart. Freeze until firm, about 30 minutes.

3. Preheat oven to 350°F. Bake cookies, rotating sheets halfway through, until edges are golden, 17 to 20 minutes. Let cool 5 minutes; transfer to wire racks to cool completely. (Cookies can be stored in an airtight container at room temperature up to 3 days.)

TIP

This recipe calls for golden syrup, a thick amber liquid made from cane sugar that's authentic to Australian ginger nuts. We like Lyle's Golden Syrup, available online or at specialty food markets. We recommend giving it a try, but if you can't find it, substitute honey.

Caramel-Stuffed Chocolate Chip Cookies

MAKES 1 DOZEN

Stuffing a huge chocolate-packed cookie with creamy caramel may seem a bit over the top. But when it comes to cookies, we're willing to go there. The secret to baking this combination for full-on melting effect is freezing the scoops of caramel-filled dough for just 15 minutes before baking. The center then cooks more slowly, and you achieve a blissful balance of melted interiors and crispy edges. If you prefer your cookies super-chewy, let the dough freeze all the way through.

3 cups unbleached all-purpose flour

1½ cups packed light brown sugar

½ cup granulated sugar

1 teaspoon baking powder

¾ teaspoon baking soda

1 teaspoon coarse salt

2 sticks (1 cup) cold unsalted butter, cut into ½-inch pieces

2 cups (12 ounces) semisweet chocolate chips

2 large eggs, room temperature

1 teaspoon vanilla extract

18 caramels, halved

1. Preheat oven to 375°F. In a large bowl, with an electric mixer on medium, mix together flour, both sugars, baking powder, baking soda, and salt. Add butter and beat on medium until combined but some pea-size butter pieces remain. Add chocolate chips and beat until combined. Beat in eggs, one at a time, and vanilla.

2. Scoop dough into 4-ounce balls (each about ⅓ cup); make a deep, wide hollow in each center. Enclose 3 pieces of caramel in each and roll back into a ball. Transfer to parchment-lined baking sheets, spacing about 3 inches apart. Freeze until firm, about 15 minutes.

3. Bake cookies 10 minutes. Reduce heat to 350°F, rotate sheets, and continue to bake until centers are almost but not completely set (press gently on tops with your fingers to check), 7 to 10 minutes more. Bang baking sheets on a counter a few times to create cracks in tops of cookies. Transfer baking sheets to wire racks and let cool completely. (Cookies can be stored in an airtight container at room temperature up to 3 days.)

TIP

While most of our recipes call for butter to be at room temperature, this cookie requires cold butter, as it would be if you were making a pie crust. The butter is then coated with flour as you mix the ingredients, which results in a more tender cookie.

Breakfast Cookies to Share

MAKES 10 LARGE OR 20 MEDIUM COOKIES

A cookie for breakfast? Yes, if it's one of these giant granola-like versions, packed with nuts, fruits, and seeds, perfect for coffee and friends. (But we won't tell if you keep it just for yourself.) They're inspired by the ones Randell Dodge, owner of Red Barn Bakery, bakes for the Bedford Farmers' Market.

2 cups whole-wheat flour

2 cups unbleached all-purpose flour

1½ teaspoons baking soda

½ teaspoon coarse salt

4 sticks (2 cups) unsalted butter, room temperature

3 cups packed dark brown sugar

4 large eggs, room temperature

1 tablespoon plus 1 teaspoon vanilla extract

4 cups old-fashioned rolled oats

1 cup raw almonds, coarsely chopped

½ cup raw pumpkin seeds

½ cup raw sunflower seeds

½ cup unsweetened shredded coconut

½ cup raisins or currants

½ cup finely chopped dried mango

½ cup finely chopped dried papaya

1 cup banana chips

1. Preheat oven to 350°F. In a large bowl, whisk together both flours, baking soda, and salt.

2. In another large bowl, with an electric mixer on medium, beat butter until pale and fluffy, about 3 minutes. Beat in sugar until well combined. Add eggs, one at a time, beating well after each addition. Beat in vanilla until just combined.

3. Gradually add flour mixture and mix on low until just combined. Add oats, almonds, both seeds, coconut, raisins, mango, and papaya, and mix to combine.

4. Scoop dough into 8 cookies (1 cup each) or 16 cookies (½ cup each). Transfer to parchment-lined baking sheets (2 large or 4 medium cookies per sheet), spacing about 3 inches apart. Top with banana chips, gently pressing down to adhere.

5. Bake cookies, rotating halfway through, until golden and firm, 20 to 25 minutes. Let cool completely on baking sheets, 25 to 30 minutes. (Cookies can be stored in an airtight container at room temperature up to 1 week.)

TIP

Be sure to use unsweetened coconut in these cookies, as the dried fruit and brown sugar provide enough sweetness.

Giant White-Chocolate Pecan Cookies

MAKES ABOUT 10

This crisp-chewy, oversized treat will give you a lot to love. White chocolate, made from cocoa butter, milk, and sugar, supplies some extra sweet notes. Its name is a little misleading—white chocolate isn't technically "chocolate," since it contains no cacao solids. We recommend using a high-quality white chocolate for delicate, creamy pockets of goodness.

1¾ cups unbleached all-purpose flour

1 teaspoon coarse salt

1 teaspoon baking soda

1 stick (½ cup) plus 6 tablespoons unsalted butter, room temperature

1¼ cups packed dark brown sugar

¼ cup plus 2 tablespoons granulated sugar

1 large egg, plus 1 large egg yolk, room temperature

1½ teaspoons vanilla extract

8 ounces white chocolate, chopped into ½- to ¾-inch pieces

8 ounces pecans, toasted (see page 248) and coarsely chopped

1. Preheat oven to 350°F. In a medium bowl, whisk together flour, salt, and baking soda to combine.

2. In a large bowl, with an electric mixer on medium, beat butter and both sugars until pale and fluffy, about 4 minutes. Beat in egg, then egg yolk, until thoroughly incorporated. Beat in vanilla. With a mixer on low, gradually add flour mixture, beating until just combined. Beat in white chocolate and pecans until just combined.

3. Using a 4-ounce (2¾-inch) ice cream scoop, drop scoops of the dough onto parchment-lined baking sheets (2 scoops per sheet), spacing 3 inches apart. Gently press to flatten.

4. Bake cookies, rotating sheets halfway through, until golden but still soft in center, about 14 minutes. Let cool slightly on baking sheets. Serve warm, or transfer cookies to wire racks to cool completely. (Cookies can be stored in an airtight container at room temperature up to 3 days.)

Big Almond–Orange Ginger Cookie

SERVES 8 TO 10

A citrusy, streusel-topped bar cookie can be as large as you'd like, and cut into generous pie-like wedges or squares. Here, the streusel does double duty as both crust and topping. Meaning "something strewn" in Old German, streusel can be tossed together in a minute, yet adds so much to the finished dessert.

1 stick (½ cup) plus 6 tablespoons unsalted butter, room temperature, plus more for pan

1¾ cups unbleached all-purpose flour

1 teaspoon coarse salt

¼ teaspoon ground cardamom

1½ cups (7½ ounces) blanched almonds, toasted (see page 248) and finely ground

¾ cup orange marmalade

2 tablespoons fresh lemon juice

⅔ cup sugar

½ teaspoon grated orange zest

1 teaspoon grated peeled fresh ginger (from a 1-inch piece)

1. Preheat oven to 350°F. Butter bottom and sides of an 8-by-11-inch tart pan with a removable bottom (see Tip). In a medium bowl, whisk together flour, salt, and cardamom. Whisk in ground almonds.

2. In a small bowl, stir together marmalade and lemon juice.

3. In a large bowl, with an electric mixer on medium, beat butter with sugar, orange zest, and ginger until pale and fluffy, about 3 minutes. Gradually add flour mixture and mix on low just until clumps begin to form, about 30 seconds. Press 3 packed cups of mixture into bottom and up sides of prepared pan. Spread marmalade mixture over crust. Crumble remaining flour–butter mixture over top, creating clumps.

4. Bake 25 minutes. Reduce heat to 300°F, rotate pan, and continue baking until light golden brown and firm, 25 to 30 minutes. Transfer pan to a wire rack and let cool completely. Remove cookie from pan, running a spatula between cookie and base to release. (Store cookie in an airtight container at room temperature up to 2 days.)

TIP

You can also make this in a 10-inch springform pan.

Scottish Shortbread

MAKES ONE 8-INCH ROUND

A couple of ingredients are key to these "butter biscuits." Rice flour
has long been the secret of Scottish bakers for making shortbread with
the perfect sandy texture. And with such a short ingredient list, it's
important to use the best-quality salted butter you can find—it adds that
distinct flavor and balances the sweetness. Shortbread keeps well
in an airtight container, and its flavor even improves after a few days.

1½ sticks (¾ cup) salted butter, room temperature, plus more for mold (see Tip)

¾ cup superfine sugar

1¾ cups unbleached all-purpose flour

¼ cup white rice flour

1. Preheat oven to 300°F. Butter an 8-inch fluted tart pan with a removable bottom, or a pie dish. In a large bowl, with an electric mixer on medium, beat butter and sugar until well combined. Add both flours and mix on low until just combined and a shaggy dough forms.

2. Firmly press dough into pan in an even layer. Cut a round from center using a 1½-inch cookie cutter; discard. Place cutter back in center. Using a sharp knife, cut shortbread into wedges. Using a fork, prick the dough to prevent shortbread from bubbling as it bakes. Bake until edges just begin to turn golden, about 1 hour, 15 minutes, checking at 1 hour. Remove from oven; turn oven off. Let shortbread cool in pan, 10 minutes.

3. Separate wedges, recutting if necessary, then return sheet to off oven until shortbread is dry, at least 1 hour. Transfer sheet to wire rack and let cool completely. (Shortbread can be stored in an airtight container at room temperature up to 2 weeks.)

TIP

Use a European or European-style butter with a high butterfat percentage, such as Kerrygold.

Jumbo Oatmeal Raisin Cookies

MAKES 8

When we supersized the classic oatmeal cookie, we made room for three different kinds of raisins: dark, golden, and Monukka. Large and rich in flavor, the Monukka variety proves to be a pleasing addition; but if you have trouble finding it, simply use 1½ cups each dark and golden raisins.

2 cups unbleached all-purpose flour

1½ teaspoons coarse salt

1 teaspoon ground cinnamon

1 teaspoon baking soda

½ teaspoon baking powder

2 sticks (1 cup) unsalted butter, room temperature

¾ cup granulated sugar

¾ cup packed light brown sugar

2 large eggs, room temperature

1 tablespoon vanilla extract

2 cups old-fashioned rolled oats

3 cups raisins, preferably a mixture of dark, golden, and Monukka

1. Preheat oven to 350°F. In a medium bowl, whisk together flour, salt, cinnamon, baking soda, and baking powder. In a large bowl, with an electric mixer on medium, beat butter and both sugars until pale and fluffy, about 2 minutes. With mixer on low, beat in eggs, one at a time, and then vanilla. Gradually add flour mixture and mix on low until well combined. Mix in oats and raisins until just combined.

2. Scoop dough into 8 balls (¾ cup each). Transfer to parchment-lined baking sheets, spacing about 3 inches apart. Use the palm of your hand to flatten into 4-inch rounds. Bake cookies, rotating sheets halfway through, until golden brown, about 16 minutes. Let cool 2 minutes. Transfer cookies to wire racks to cool completely. (Cookies can be stored in an airtight container up to 3 days.)

TIP

If you want to swap out the raisins for another dried fruit, cranberries, sour cherries, or diced apricots could stand in nicely.

Extraordinary Chocolate Chip Cookies

MAKES 14

More than four cups of chocolate chips put this cookie in the extra-special, extra-chocolatey category. It has just the right proportion of sugar to flour and butter, which results in crisp edges and delightfully chewy centers. It's everything a chocolate chip cookie should be, and then some.

2¾ cups unbleached all-purpose flour

1¼ teaspoons coarse salt

1 teaspoon baking powder

1 teaspoon baking soda

2½ sticks (1¼ cups) unsalted butter, room temperature

1¼ cups packed dark brown sugar

¾ cup granulated sugar

2 large eggs, room temperature

1 teaspoon vanilla extract

4½ cups semisweet chocolate chips

1. In a medium bowl, whisk together flour, salt, baking powder, and baking soda.

2. In a large bowl, with an electric mixer on medium, beat butter and both sugars until pale and fluffy, about 4 minutes. Beat in eggs, one at a time; add vanilla. With mixer on low, gradually add flour mixture; beat until just combined. Add chocolate chips; mix until evenly distributed throughout. Refrigerate dough at least 1 hour and up to overnight.

3. Preheat oven to 350°F. Using a 4-ounce (2¾-inch) ice cream scoop, drop dough onto parchment-lined baking sheets, about 2 inches apart. Bake cookies, rotating sheets halfway through, until golden around the edges, 15 to 17 minutes. Let cool 5 minutes. Transfer cookies to wire racks to cool completely. (Cookies can be stored in an airtight container at room temperature for 3 days.)

TIP

Chilling dough overnight results in a more concentrated sweetness and prevents the cookie from spreading too thin when baked. Why? Because the chilled, solidified butter takes longer to melt, hence longer to spread; the dough is also drier, and sugar breaks down for a deeply sweet treat.

Everyday Celebration Cookies

MAKES 4

Perfect for birthdays, anniversaries, or any momentous occasion, this cakey cookie is topped with fluffy vanilla buttercream and colorful nonpareils. Play with different variations—we also loved how sugar pearls looked (see page 256) and how chocolate frosting tasted (just beat 6 ounces melted and cooled bittersweet chocolate into the Basic Buttercream recipe). With so many options, why wait for a special event? The cookie itself is something to celebrate.

2½ cups unbleached all-purpose flour

1¼ teaspoons coarse salt

2 teaspoons baking powder

1 stick (½ cup) unsalted butter, room temperature

½ cup cream cheese, room temperature

1½ cups packed light brown sugar

2 large eggs, room temperature

2 teaspoons vanilla extract

½ recipe Basic Buttercream (page 245)

Multicolored nonpareils, for decorating

1. In a medium bowl, whisk together flour, salt, and baking powder. In a large bowl, with a mixer on medium-high, beat butter, cream cheese, and sugar until pale and fluffy, 2 to 3 minutes, scraping down sides of bowl with a rubber spatula as necessary. Add eggs and vanilla, beating until combined. With mixer on low, gradually beat in flour mixture until just combined. Shape dough into a disk 1 inch thick, wrap tightly in plastic, and refrigerate until firm, at least 2 hours and up to 3 days.

2. Preheat oven to 350°F. Divide dough evenly into 4 rounds and roll, or press using your flattened palms, into ½-inch-thick circles. Transfer to parchment-lined baking sheets, spacing 2 inches apart.

3. Bake cookies, rotating sheets halfway through, until puffed and set but still soft when gently pressed in the center, 15 to 18 minutes. Transfer cookies to wire racks and let cool completely. Using a small offset spatula, frost with buttercream in gentle swoops; immediately sprinkle with nonpareils before frosting sets. (Cookies are best eaten the day they are made.)

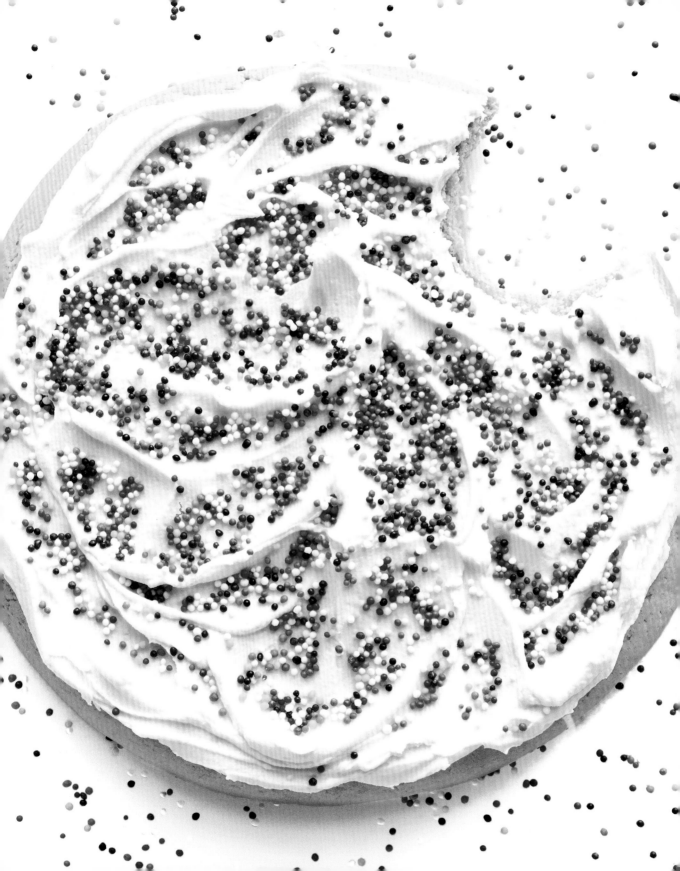

5

TOOLS OF THE TRADE

With a little help from molds and spritzes,
rolling pins and textured mats, and even
a meat mallet, these cookies take on designs,
graphics, and whimsical appeal.

Walnut Cookies

MAKES ABOUT 2 DOZEN

We took these cookies to a fantastically indulgent level. First we added walnut liqueur to the cookie dough, and then shaped it with a springerle mold into edible walnuts. Sandwiched between the cookie shells is a luxurious chocolate filling mixed with (what else?) toasted walnuts.

FOR THE COOKIES

2½ cups unbleached all-purpose flour

½ teaspoon coarse salt

½ teaspoon ground cinnamon

¼ teaspoon ground ginger

1½ sticks (¾ cup) unsalted butter, room temperature

3 ounces cream cheese, softened

½ cup granulated sugar

½ cup packed light brown sugar

1 large egg yolk, room temperature

1 tablespoon walnut liqueur

Confectioners' sugar, sifted, for mold

FOR THE FILLING

6 tablespoons unsalted butter, room temperature

1 cup confectioners' sugar, sifted

½ cup walnuts, toasted (see page 248) and finely chopped

Pinch of coarse salt

5 ounces semisweet chocolate, melted (see page 248) and slightly cooled

1. Make the cookies: In a medium bowl, whisk together flour, salt, cinnamon, and ginger. In a large bowl, with an electric mixer on medium, beat butter, cream cheese, and granulated and brown sugars until pale and fluffy, about 2 minutes. Beat in egg yolk and walnut liqueur. With mixer on low, gradually add flour mixture, beating until just combined. Form dough into a 1-inch-thick disk, wrap in plastic, and refrigerate for 1 hour.

2. Using a fine-mesh sieve, generously dust a walnut springerle mold with confectioners' sugar. Cut a piece of dough about the size of the mold. Press dough into mold with fingers, working from center. Gently coax dough out of mold with fingertips and transfer with an offset spatula to a baking sheet. Repeat, spacing cookies 1 inch apart on parchment-lined sheets and cleaning mold often. Freeze cookies for 1 hour.

3. Preheat oven to 325°F. Bake cookies, rotating sheets halfway through, until set, 25 to 30 minutes. Transfer baking sheets to wire racks and let cool completely.

4. Make the filling: With an electric mixer on medium, beat butter and confectioners' sugar until pale and fluffy, about 3 minutes. Beat in walnuts and salt until combined. Beat in chocolate.

5. Pipe or spread 1 teaspoon filling on flat side of one cookie. Press flat side of another cookie onto filling to sandwich. Repeat with remaining cookies and filling. (Cookies can be stored in an airtight container at room temperature up to 2 days.)

Stroopwafels

MAKES ABOUT 1 DOZEN

Two waffle cookies pressed together with caramel, *stroopwafels* ("syrup waffles") are a favorite snack in the Netherlands, where they are often placed on top of hot drinks to keep the cookies warm and to melt the caramel. You'll need a waffle-cone maker to prepare them, but if you love ice cream, that special equipment will do double duty. Waffle-cone makers look and work just like electric waffle irons; or you can use a cialde iron, the same tool used to cook Pizzelles (see page 160).

FOR THE WAFFLES

1¼ cups unbleached all-purpose flour

1 teaspoon baking powder

¼ teaspoon coarse salt

2 large eggs, room temperature

¾ cup sugar

2 teaspoons vanilla extract

½ teaspoon lemon extract

⅓ cup unsalted butter, melted and cooled

FOR THE FILLING

1 cup sugar

1 tablespoon light corn syrup

⅓ cup heavy cream

1 vanilla bean, split and seeds scraped

1 tablespoon unsalted butter

½ teaspoon coarse salt

1. Make the waffles: Heat an electric nonstick waffle-cone iron. In a medium bowl, whisk together flour, baking powder, and salt.

2. In a large bowl, whisk eggs. Whisk in sugar until well combined; whisk in both extracts. While whisking, slowly add cooled butter in a steady stream until batter is smooth. Add flour mixture and whisk until thoroughly combined. Transfer batter to a large pastry bag fitted with a ½-inch round tip (such as Ateco #806). Pipe batter into a 2-inch circle in center of heated waffle-cone iron. Close lid and lock with clasp. Cook until golden brown, 1½ to 2 minutes. Using a small offset spatula, remove waffle and immediately transfer to a cutting board. Using a 3½-inch round cutter, cut out cookies; let cool completely on a wire rack. Repeat.

3. Make the filling: Combine sugar, corn syrup, and ¼ cup water in a medium saucepan. Without stirring, cook, carefully swirling, until sugar dissolves. Continue to cook without stirring, carefully swirling, until dark amber in color, about 10 minutes. Reduce heat to low and slowly add cream, stirring with a wooden spoon until combined. Add vanilla seeds, butter, and salt; stir until caramel is smooth. Strain through a fine-mesh sieve into a heatproof bowl; set aside to cool slightly.

4. Spread caramel filling onto bottoms of half the cookies, then sandwich with remaining cookies, pressing to spread filling to edges. (Filled cookies can be stored in an airtight container at room temperature up to 3 days.)

Iranian Rice Cookies

MAKES ABOUT 16

These crumbly rice-flour cookies, called *nan-e berenji*, are made using cardamom and a sugar syrup infused with rose water, a classic ingredient in Middle Eastern sweets. One of the most traditional cookies in Persian culture, they're served at special occasions, from the celebration of the New Year (Norouz) to weddings. Here, the textured end of a meat mallet is gently pressed into the dough to form a grid pattern.

1½ sticks (¾ cup) unsalted butter

¼ cup sugar

⅛ teaspoon rose water

1 large egg yolk

½ cup unbleached all-purpose flour

¾ cup white rice flour, plus more for dusting

½ teaspoon ground cardamom, preferably fresh

½ teaspoon coarse salt

1. Preheat oven to 350°F. Line a fine-mesh sieve with 4 layers of cheesecloth; set over a small liquid measuring cup. Melt butter in a small saucepan over medium-high heat until beginning to boil. Reduce heat to medium and simmer until foamy, stirring occasionally, until butter turns golden brown with a nutty aroma, and milk solids separate into brown specks that sink to bottom, 5 to 7 minutes. Remove saucepan from heat and strain butter through prepared sieve, leaving solids behind. Let cool slightly.

2. In another small saucepan over medium heat, stir together sugar and 2 tablespoons water until sugar has dissolved; transfer to a large bowl. Let cool slightly. Add rose water and stir to combine.

3. Add egg yolk to sugar mixture; whisk until light and slightly thickened. Continue whisking and drizzle in strained brown butter until thick and incorporated. In a medium bowl, whisk together both flours, the cardamom, and salt. Add to brown butter mixture and stir until incorporated.

4. Roll or scoop dough into 1½-inch balls and place about 1 inch apart on parchment-lined baking sheets. Imprint each ball with the grooved side of a meat mallet, pressing to ¼ inch thick. Dust mallet with rice flour as needed to prevent sticking. Bake, rotating sheets halfway through, until edges of cookies just turn light golden, 16 to 18 minutes. Transfer cookies to wire racks to cool completely. (Cookies can be stored in an airtight container at room temperature up to 3 days.)

Chocolate-Dipped Bear Paws

MAKES 2 DOZEN

Our bear paws may look like madeleines, a cakey treat, but they are actually crisp cookies. We've updated the original Czech classic, with its ground nuts and warm spices, by dipping it in melted bittersweet chocolate. To bake these cookies in one batch, you will need two madeleine pans. You can also bake them in two batches, cooling and buttering the pan between uses.

2 sticks (1 cup) unsalted butter, room temperature, plus more for pans

¾ cup sugar

2½ cups unbleached all-purpose flour

1 teaspoon ground cinnamon

¼ teaspoon ground cloves

½ teaspoon coarse salt

4 ounces almonds, toasted (see page 248) and finely ground (see Tip)

6 ounces bittersweet chocolate, chopped and melted (see page 248)

1. In a medium bowl, with an electric mixer on medium-high, beat butter and sugar until pale and fluffy, about 2 minutes. Add flour, spices, salt, and almonds, and beat on low until dough starts to come together, about 1 minute. Cover bowl with plastic wrap and refrigerate until firm, about 1 hour.

2. Preheat oven to 350°F. Brush 2 madeleine pans with butter. Press 2 packed table-spoons of dough into each mold (dough should be level with top of the mold). Bake cookies, rotating pans halfway through, until edges are brown, about 20 minutes. Transfer pans to wire racks and let cool 10 minutes. Invert pans over racks and tap to release the cookies from the mold. Let cool completely.

3. Dip each cookie on the diagonal into melted chocolate, then place on a parchment-lined baking sheet. Refrigerate until chocolate is set, about 30 minutes. (Dipped cookies can be stored, covered, in the refrigerator up to 3 days; undipped cookies can be stored in an airtight container at room temperature up to 1 week.)

TIP

The best way to finely grind toasted almonds is in your food processor, pulsing to check on consistency. Too long in the processor will turn the nuts and their oils into almond butter.

Speculaas

MAKES ABOUT 2 DOZEN

One of the most popular Dutch treats is a spice-filled, crunchy cookie called *speculaas*, or "mirror," since it reflects the image of the carved wooden (or, more common today, earthenware) mold from which it's shaped. To follow custom, use molds of windmills or figures in traditional Dutch clothing. But feel free to "break the mold" and use any cookie cutter you please; just roll out the dough to ¼ inch thick.

3 cups unbleached all-purpose flour, plus more for dusting

½ teaspoon baking soda

1 teaspoon coarse salt

2 teaspoons ground cinnamon

1½ teaspoons freshly grated nutmeg

1 teaspoon freshly ground cardamom

1 teaspoon ground coriander

1 teaspoon ground ginger

½ teaspoon ground cloves

¼ teaspoon freshly ground mace

¼ teaspoon freshly ground white pepper

1½ sticks (¾ cup) unsalted butter, room temperature

1 cup packed dark brown sugar

½ cup granulated sugar

⅓ cup whole milk

1. In a medium bowl, whisk together flour, baking soda, salt, and spices. In a large bowl, with an electric mixer on medium, beat butter and both sugars until pale and fluffy, about 2 minutes. Add half the flour mixture and mix on low until just combined. Mix in milk, followed by remaining flour mixture. Shape dough into a disk, wrap in plastic, and refrigerate until firm, at least 2 hours and up to overnight.

2. Dab speculaas mold all over with a small piece of dough (the buttery coating helps prevent sticking). Generously sprinkle mold with flour, tapping to remove excess. Take a piece of dough roughly the same size as mold; using your palm, press into mold. Using a thin knife, scrape off excess dough. Invert mold over parchment-lined baking sheets; rap far end of mold against sheet, holding it at an angle to release cookie. Sprinkle mold with flour; repeat with remaining dough. Gather scraps (refrigerate if too soft) and form more cookies. Freeze at least 30 minutes.

3. Preheat oven to 350°F. Bake cookies, rotating sheets halfway through, until firm and golden, 15 to 20 minutes. Transfer parchment with cookies to wire racks and let cool completely. (Cookies can be stored in an airtight container at room temperature up to 3 days.)

TIP

Be sure to flour the speculaas mold, to prevent the dough from sticking.

Spiced Cardamom Cookies

MAKES 5 DOZEN

No icing or other embellishment is needed for these lightly spicy treats, which are a cross between gingerbread cookies and animal crackers. They get their character instead from their charming wood-grain texture. To re-create them, you can use a faux-bois mat or a rolling pin with a textured surface. Make the dough a day before you plan to bake the cookies.

5¾ cups unbleached all-purpose flour, plus more for dusting

1 teaspoon baking soda

1 tablespoon coarse salt

1 tablespoon ground cardamom

1 teaspoon ground allspice

¼ teaspoon freshly ground pepper

¼ teaspoon ground cloves

2 sticks (1 cup) unsalted butter, cut into pieces and room temperature

1 cup packed dark brown sugar

½ cup granulated sugar

½ cup dark corn syrup

¼ cup heavy cream, room temperature

1 large egg, room temperature

1½ teaspoons vanilla extract

---

1. In a large bowl, whisk together flour, baking soda, salt, cardamom, allspice, pepper, and cloves. Place butter in another large bowl. In a large saucepan, bring both sugars, corn syrup, and ¼ cup water to a boil, stirring until sugar dissolves. Pour hot sugar mixture over butter. With an electric mixer on low, beat until combined.

2. Add cream, egg, and vanilla, and with mixer on medium, beat until well combined. With mixer on low, gradually add flour mixture, beating until just incorporated. Shape dough into 3 disks and wrap in plastic. Refrigerate overnight (or freeze up to 1 month; thaw in the refrigerator before using).

3. Preheat oven to 350°F. Working with one disk at a time, roll out between lightly floured parchment to ⅛-inch thickness. Place a lightly floured faux-bois mat on dough, pattern side down. With rolling pin, lightly roll over mat to imprint dough. Carefully remove mat. Transfer dough on parchment to a baking sheet and refrigerate until firm, about 10 minutes. Repeat with remaining disks.

4. Using a sharp paring knife, cut out shapes to mimic wood chips about 1½ by 3 inches. Transfer cookies to parchment-lined baking sheets, spacing about 1 inch apart. Roll out and cut scraps once. Bake cookies until edges are golden brown, 10 to 12 minutes, rotating sheets halfway through. Transfer to wire racks and let cool. (Cookies can be stored in an airtight container at room temperature up to 2 weeks.)

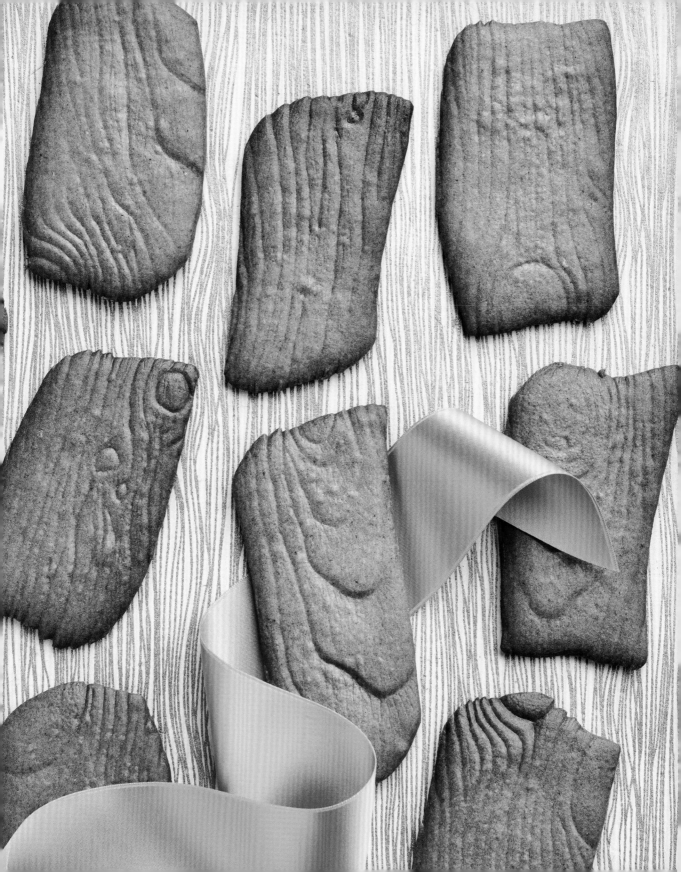

Danish Butter Cookies

MAKES ABOUT 20

In Denmark, where these ring-shaped Christmas cookies were created in the 1840s, they are commonly known as *vaniljekranse* ("vanilla wreaths"). They're a good excuse to splurge on a European butter with a high butterfat content. It gives the cookies a softer texture and richer flavor. The Danes have always used salted butter, so our recipe follows that tradition.

2 sticks (1 cup) best-quality salted butter, room temperature

1 cup confectioners' sugar, sifted

1 teaspoon vanilla extract

1 large egg, room temperature

2½ cups unbleached all-purpose flour

1. Preheat oven to 325°F. In a large bowl, with an electric mixer on medium, beat butter and sugar until pale and fluffy, about 3 minutes. Add vanilla and egg, and beat to combine. Gradually add flour, beating until well incorporated. Transfer dough to a pastry bag fitted with a $^7/_{16}$-inch star tip (such as Ateco #825).

2. Pipe 2½-inch rings onto parchment-lined baking sheets, about 2 inches apart. Bake cookies, rotating sheets halfway through, until lightly golden around edges but still light on top, about 20 minutes. Transfer sheets to wire racks and let cool completely. (Cookies can be stored in an airtight container at room temperature up to 3 days.)

TIPS

Beginning with room-temperature ingredients creates a more easily piped dough. As we recommend when piping meringues, dab a little dough between the parchment and baking sheet in each corner to hold the paper in place. And when piping, don't put all the dough in the pastry bag in one go. A smaller amount gives you better control.

Pizzelles

MAKES ABOUT 20

According to some culinary historians, the crisp Italian wafer cookie known as the *pizzelle* has been around since the eighth century, making it one of the world's oldest. Pizzelle batter is cooked on a special pan (cialde iron), which gives the cookies decorative patterns. It was once common for the irons to be customized to reflect a family's crest. We've made our pizzelles (kissed with anise) into pretty snowflakes, dusted, as is customary, with confectioners' sugar.

1¼ teaspoons anise seeds

1¼ cups unbleached all-purpose flour

½ teaspoon baking powder

½ teaspoon coarse salt

2 large eggs, room temperature

¾ cup granulated sugar

1 teaspoon vanilla extract

1 teaspoon anise extract

5 tablespoons unsalted butter, melted and cooled

Confectioners' sugar, sifted (optional)

1. Heat a nonstick pizzelle iron. In a small skillet, toast anise seeds over high heat, stirring, until fragrant, about 1 minute. Transfer seeds to a spice grinder, let cool, and finely grind. Scrape into a medium bowl; whisk together with flour, baking powder, and salt.

2. In a large bowl, whisk eggs and granulated sugar until well combined. Whisk in vanilla and anise extracts. Slowly add cooled butter in a steady stream, whisking continuously, until batter is smooth. Stir in flour mixture until just combined (do not overmix).

3. Transfer batter to a pastry bag fitted with a ½-inch round tip (such as Ateco #806). Pipe about 2 tablespoons batter in a circle around the center of each pattern on the heated pizzelle iron. Close and seal with clasp. Cook until golden brown, about 45 seconds.

4. Using a small spatula, release and remove cookies. Using kitchen shears or a 4½-inch ring mold, trim any ragged edges, if desired. Transfer cookies to a wire rack to cool. Repeat with remaining batter. Dust cooled cookies with confectioners' sugar, if desired. (Cookies can be stored in an airtight container at room temperature up to 2 weeks.)

Brown-Butter Honey Cookies

MAKES ABOUT 5 DOZEN

Just a few touches take this cookie from plain to extraordinary. Brown butter gives it a lovely nutty flavor, a small amount of cardamom adds just enough spice, and rolling the dough with an embossed rolling pin supplies a beautiful pattern. The pins come in a wide variety of designs—basket weave as shown here, flowers, even whimsical cats and dogs.

1 stick (½ cup) unsalted butter

2¾ cups unbleached all-purpose flour, plus more for dusting

1 teaspoon ground cardamom

½ teaspoon coarse salt

½ cup packed dark brown sugar

¼ cup granulated sugar

¼ cup honey

2 tablespoons heavy cream

1 large egg yolk

1 teaspoon vanilla extract

1. Melt butter in a small saucepan over medium heat and cook, swirling pan occasionally, until golden brown, 3 to 5 minutes; transfer brown butter to heatproof bowl and cool until solid.

2. In a large bowl, whisk together flour, cardamom, and salt. In another large bowl, with an electric mixer on medium, beat brown butter and both sugars until pale and fluffy, about 3 minutes. Add honey, cream, egg yolk, and vanilla. Continue beating until well combined, about 1 minute more.

Gradually add flour mixture and mix on low until just combined. Divide dough into 4 equal pieces and cover with plastic wrap.

3. Preheat oven to 325°F. Working with one piece of dough at a time, roll out on lightly floured parchment to ⅛-inch thickness. Roll with a textured rolling pin to imprint. Using a 2½-inch square cutter, cut out cookies and transfer to parchment-lined baking sheets. Repeat with remaining dough, rerolling the scraps one time. Freeze until solid, about 15 minutes.

4. Transfer chilled cookies to fresh parchment-lined baking sheets, spacing about 1 inch apart. Bake cookies, rotating sheets halfway through, until lightly golden brown, 16 to 18 minutes. Transfer cookies to wire racks to cool completely. (Cookies can be stored in an airtight container at room temperature up to 2 weeks.)

PERFECTING
SPRITZ COOKIES

Think of the spritz (both the basic vanilla dough and the method) as the starting point for endless variations. It's a multitasker in the best way possible. Mini tweaks to the basic recipe—hints of spices or a dash of cocoa or a touch of citrus zest—and an assortment of cookie-press disks to craft all kinds of shapes offer you a world of cookies. That's what we call smart baking.

MAKES ABOUT 4 DOZEN

3 cups unbleached all-purpose flour

½ teaspoon coarse salt

2 sticks (1 cup) unsalted butter, room temperature

1 cup granulated sugar

1 large egg, room temperature

2 teaspoons vanilla extract

Citrus and/or Vanilla Glaze (recipes follow)

Sanding sugar, for sprinkling (optional)

1. Whisk together flour and salt in a large bowl. In another large bowl, with an electric mixer on medium-high, beat butter and granulated sugar until pale and fluffy, about 3 minutes. Beat in egg and vanilla. Gradually add flour mixture and mix on low until just combined. (At this point, dough can be refrigerated overnight or frozen up to 1 month.)

2. Preheat oven to 350°F and chill baking sheets (see Tips on page 166). Knead dough briefly to soften. Fill a cookie press with dough and fit with disk to make shapes. Squeeze cookies directly onto chilled baking sheets. Bake cookies until firm, 12 to 14 minutes. Transfer cookies to wire racks and let cool completely.

3. Dip cookies, face down, into glaze. Sprinkle with sanding sugar, if desired. Transfer to a wire rack set over parchment and let set, about 10 minutes. (Cookies can be stored in an airtight container at room temperature up to 5 days.)

Citrus Glaze

Combine 3 cups sifted confectioners' sugar, ¼ cup plus 2 tablespoons fresh citrus juice (such as lemon or orange), 3 teaspoons finely grated citrus zest, and 3 tablespoons light corn syrup in a medium bowl. Whisk until smooth.

Vanilla Glaze

Combine 3 cups sifted confectioners' sugar, ¼ cup plus 2 tablespoons whole milk, 3 tablespoons light corn syrup, and 1 teaspoon vanilla extract in a medium bowl. Whisk until smooth.

SPRITZ VARIATIONS

Chocolate Dough

Replace ⅓ cup flour with ⅓ cup unsweetened Dutch-process cocoa powder.

Citrus Dough

Replace vanilla extract with 1 teaspoon finely grated citrus zest and 1 tablespoon fresh citrus juice (such as lemon or orange).

Spiced Dough

Add 1½ teaspoons ground cinnamon, ¼ teaspoon ground ginger, ¼ teaspoon ground allspice, and ¼ teaspoon freshly ground pepper when you add flour mixture.

Tips for Spritz

• Cold, unlined, and ungreased baking sheets will help the cookies retain their shape; they won't spread while baking.

• Make sure the butter is on the softer side of room temperature. The dough should be fairly soft and supple for squeezing through the press.

• For a light, crisp cookie, cream the butter mixture well—both before and after the egg is added—and don't overmix after adding the flour.

• A cookie press fitted with a disk is the secret tool to making these beautiful shapes. Hold the filled cookie press directly against the baking sheet and press the dough through the holes. You can change the disks at any time for different shapes.

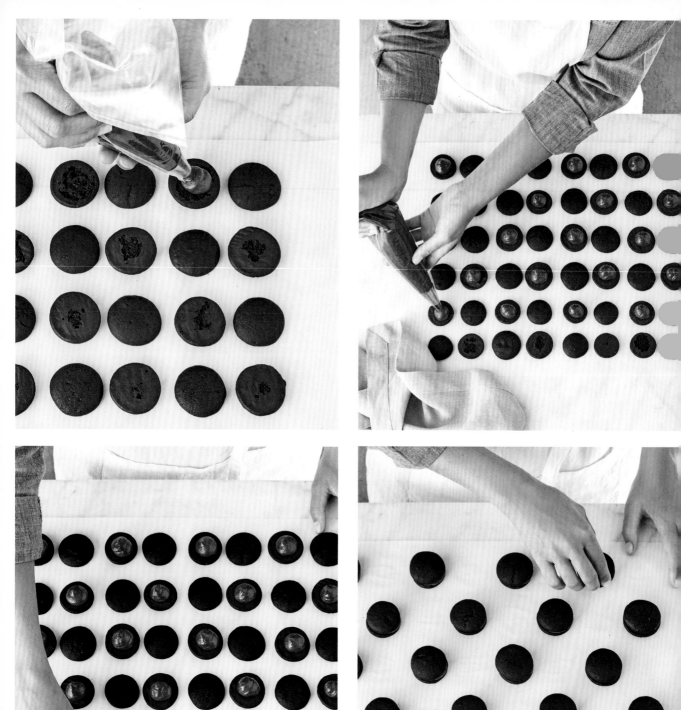

6

COOKIES BY ANY OTHER NAME

Puffy whoopie pies; chewy, cakey,
or fudgy brownies; fruit-packed bars; and
lush chocolate truffles—call them
whatever you like, they're still among the
best sweet treats we know.

Mini Chocolate Whoopie Pies

MAKES ABOUT 32

There are a lot of stories about where the whoopie pie first came into being—from Maine to Massachusetts to Pennsylvania Dutch Country. Whatever its origins, this sandwich of fluffy cake with creamy filling has taken its place in the hearts (and lunch boxes) of cookie and cake lovers everywhere, in myriad forms. Here, we've made them small in size and big in chocolate flavor.

FOR THE COOKIES

1¾ cups unbleached all-purpose flour

¾ cup unsweetened Dutch-process cocoa powder

1½ teaspoons baking soda

½ teaspoon coarse salt

4 tablespoons (¼ cup) unsalted butter, room temperature

½ cup granulated sugar

½ cup packed dark brown sugar

1 large egg, room temperature

1 cup whole milk

1 teaspoon vanilla extract

FOR THE WHIPPED GANACHE

8 ounces semisweet or bittersweet chocolate

1 cup heavy cream

⅛ teaspoon coarse salt

1. Make the cookies: Preheat oven to 375°F. Whisk together flour, cocoa, baking soda, and salt in a medium bowl. In another medium bowl, beat butter and both sugars with an electric mixer on high until smooth, about 3 minutes. Add egg and beat until mixture is pale and fluffy, about 3 minutes.

2. With mixer on low, add flour mixture in 2 additions, alternating with milk and vanilla, beginning and ending with flour; mix until just combined.

3. Transfer dough to a pastry bag fitted with a ½-inch round tip (such as Ateco #806). Pipe dough (about 2 teaspoons per cookie) onto parchment-lined baking sheets, spacing about 2 inches apart. Bake, rotating sheets halfway through, until cookies spring back when lightly pressed, 12 to 14 minutes. Transfer sheets to wire racks and let cool completely.

4. Make the whipped ganache: Coarsely chop chocolate with a serrated knife and place in a large heatproof bowl. In a small saucepan, bring cream just to a boil over medium-high heat. Pour over chocolate and add salt. Let stand for 10 minutes; then stir. Let ganache cool, 45 to 60 minutes, stirring occasionally. With an electric mixer on medium-high, beat ganache until pale and fluffy, 2 to 4 minutes.

5. Transfer whipped ganache to a pastry bag fitted with the ½-inch tip. Pipe ganache (2 to 2½ teaspoons per cookie) onto flat sides of half the cookies. Sandwich with remaining cookies, pressing gently. (Whoopie pies can be refrigerated in an airtight container up to 3 days.)

Lemon–Date Bars

MAKES 2 DOZEN

Medjools are known as the "king of dates" because they outshine all other varieties in size, juiciness, and natural sweetness—they're worth seeking out. Here, their caramel flavor beautifully balances the deliciously tart lemon bars that were inspired by pastry chef and cookbook author Maida Heatter. Reducing the baking temperature after the crust turns golden brown and the citrus filling is added allows the bars to set without burning the crust.

FOR THE CRUST

1½ sticks (¾ cup) unsalted butter, room temperature, cut into pieces, plus more for baking dish

1¾ cups unbleached all-purpose flour

¾ cup confectioners' sugar, sifted, plus more for dusting

1 teaspoon coarse salt

FOR THE FILLING

8 ounces Medjool dates, pitted

1 cup boiling water

1¼ cups granulated sugar

¼ cup unbleached all-purpose flour

¾ teaspoon coarse salt

4 large eggs

1 tablespoon finely grated lemon zest, plus ¾ cup fresh juice (from 4 to 5 lemons)

1. Make the crust: Preheat oven to 350°F. Butter a 9-by-13-inch baking dish and line with parchment, leaving a 2-inch overhang on 2 sides. Butter parchment. Whisk together flour, confectioners' sugar, and salt in a large bowl. Work in butter with your fingertips until combined and mixture holds together when pinched. Press crust evenly into bottom of prepared pan. Freeze 15 minutes. Bake crust until light golden brown, 20 to 25 minutes.

2. Make the filling: Meanwhile, in a heatproof bowl, soak dates in boiling water 15 minutes. Drain, reserving liquid. Puree dates in a food processor with enough soaking liquid (about ½ cup) to make a spreadable paste (about 1¼ cups).

3. While dates are soaking, whisk together the granulated sugar, flour, and salt in a medium bowl. Whisk in eggs plus lemon zest and juice.

4. Spread date paste evenly over baked crust. Return to oven and bake 4 minutes. Reduce heat to 325°F, pour lemon filling over date layer, then bake until just set, about 20 minutes more. Transfer to a wire rack and let cool 20 minutes. Run a paring knife around edges, then lift bars from dish using parchment. Let cool completely. Dust with confectioners' sugar. Cut into squares. (Bars can be refrigerated in an airtight container up to 3 days.)

Chocolate Chip Cookie Brownies

MAKES 16

When you can't decide between a cookie and a brownie, why not make both—in the same pan—for what we fondly refer to as the "brookie." We dotted our cookie dough, streusel style, over brownie batter and then baked them together for a contrasting texture of cakey and fudgy layers.

FOR THE COOKIE DOUGH

1 stick (½ cup) unsalted butter, room temperature, plus more for pan

1¾ cups unbleached all-purpose flour

½ teaspoon baking soda

½ teaspoon baking powder

¾ teaspoon coarse salt

½ cup packed light brown sugar

½ cup granulated sugar

1 large egg, room temperature

1 teaspoon vanilla extract

6 ounces bittersweet chocolate, chopped

FOR THE BROWNIE BATTER

1 stick (½ cup) unsalted butter, cut into large pieces

6 ounces bittersweet chocolate, coarsely chopped

1½ cups granulated sugar

3 large eggs, room temperature

¼ cup unsweetened Dutch-process cocoa powder

½ teaspoon coarse salt

½ cup plus 2 tablespoons unbleached all-purpose flour

1. Make the cookie dough: Preheat oven to 350°F. Butter a 9-by-13-inch baking pan and line with parchment, leaving a 2-inch overhang on long sides. In a medium bowl, whisk together flour, baking soda, baking powder, and salt.

2. In a large bowl, with an electric mixer on medium-high, beat butter and both sugars until pale and fluffy, about 5 minutes. With mixer on medium-low, beat in egg and vanilla. With mixer on low, gradually add flour mixture and beat until just incorporated. Stir in chocolate.

3. Make the brownie batter: In a medium heatproof bowl set over (not in) a pot of simmering water, melt butter and chocolate, stirring until smooth. Remove from heat; whisk in granulated sugar. Whisk in eggs, one at a time, until combined. Whisk in cocoa powder and salt. Fold in flour until combined.

4. Pour brownie batter into prepared pan, smoothing top with an offset spatula. Crumble cookie dough evenly over batter. Cover with parchment-lined foil; bake until just set, about 20 minutes. Remove foil and continue baking until golden brown and a cake tester inserted into center (avoiding chocolate chunks) comes out with moist crumbs, 27 to 30 minutes more. Transfer pan to a wire rack and let cool completely. Lift brownies from pan using parchment; cut into 16 squares. (Brownies can be stored in an airtight container at room temperature up to 3 days.)

Goose Feet

MAKES 14

Hailing from Russia, these pastry-like cookies are named for their folded shapes, which resemble webbed feet (*gusinie lapki* translates to "goose feet"). They're flavored with orange zest and vanilla bean, and owe their light, flaky texture to a beloved Russian ingredient: farmer cheese. Made from cow's milk, farmer cheese is lightly salted and has a mild tanginess. If you can't find it, substitute cottage cheese.

1¾ cups unbleached all-purpose flour, plus more for dusting

1 teaspoon baking powder

½ teaspoon coarse salt

1 cup fresh farmer cheese

1 stick (½ cup) unsalted butter, room temperature

1 vanilla bean, split lengthwise, seeds scraped

1 heaping tablespoon finely grated orange zest (from 1 orange)

⅓ cup granulated sugar

1 large egg, lightly beaten

Coarse sanding sugar, for sprinkling

1. In a medium bowl, whisk together flour, baking powder, and salt. In a large bowl, mix cheese, butter, vanilla, and orange zest with a wooden spoon until well combined. Add flour mixture to cheese mixture and stir until mixture resembles coarse crumbs. Transfer dough to a piece of plastic wrap, shape into a disk, and wrap tightly. Refrigerate 1 hour.

2. Preheat oven to 350°F. On a lightly floured surface, roll out dough to ⅛ inch thick. Using a 4-inch round cutter, cut out rounds. Gather dough scraps, reroll, and cut out more rounds.

3. Place granulated sugar in a wide shallow bowl. Working with one round at a time, brush with water, then dip in granulated sugar to coat. Fold round in half, covering sugar; fold in half again. Transfer cookies to 2 parchment-lined baking sheets. Brush tops with egg wash and sprinkle with coarse sanding sugar.

4. Bake, rotating sheets halfway through, until golden, 25 to 30 minutes. Transfer sheets to wire racks and let cool completely. (Cookies are best eaten the day they are made.)

Plum-and-Blackberry Cornmeal-Almond Crumb Bars

MAKES 1 DOZEN

These crumbly bars taste like summertime, thanks to the abundance of seasonal fruit. For the best texture, choose your fruit wisely: Ripe plums are very juicy, without much structure, so use a sturdier plum with a lower moisture content, such as yellow-fleshed Italian prune plums, and combine them with another stone fruit or berries—like these plump, sweet blackberries. Taste-test your blackberries; if they're tart, temper them with an equal amount of blueberries.

FOR THE CRUST

1 stick (½ cup) plus 5 tablespoons unsalted butter, room temperature, plus more for pan

1¾ cups unbleached all-purpose flour

¼ cup coarse cornmeal

¾ teaspoon coarse salt

1 cup sugar

¼ cup blanched almonds, toasted (see page 248) and coarsely chopped

FOR THE FILLING

12 ounces plums (about 6), preferably Italian prune variety, cut into a ½-inch dice (1¾ cups)

1 cup (4 ounces) fresh blackberries

⅔ cup sugar (or ½ cup, if plums are very sweet)

3 tablespoons unbleached all-purpose flour

1 teaspoon fresh lemon juice

¼ teaspoon freshly ground pepper

¼ teaspoon coarse salt

1. Make the crust: Preheat oven to 375°F. Butter a 9-by-13-inch baking pan. Line with parchment, leaving a 2-inch overhang on all sides; butter parchment. Whisk flour, cornmeal, and salt in a medium bowl.

2. In a large bowl, with an electric mixer on medium-high, beat butter with sugar until pale and fluffy, about 3 minutes. Scrape down sides of bowl. With mixer on low, add flour mixture; beat until dough forms clumps but does not completely hold together. Press 3 cups of dough mixture into bottom and 1 inch up sides of prepared pan. Stir chopped almonds into remaining dough mixture.

3. Make the filling: Stir together plums, blackberries, sugar, flour, lemon juice, pepper, and salt. Pour into crust. Crumble remaining crust mixture over top, squeezing to create clumps. Bake until bubbling in center and crust is golden, 1 hour to 1 hour, 10 minutes (if browning too quickly, tent with foil after about 50 minutes). Let cool 1 hour. Lift bars from pan using parchment; let cool completely, about 2 hours. Cut into 12 squares. (Bars can be refrigerated in an airtight container up to 3 days.)

Triple-Chocolate Brownie Cups

MAKES 6

Here's everything you want in a brownie, in a convenient, cookie-like package: Nestled in a shallow paper baking cup, this brownie is a sinfully good combination of bittersweet chocolate and two kinds of chocolate chips. To make squares instead of cups, bake the batter in an 8-inch square pan, lined with buttered parchment, for 35 to 40 minutes; then cut into 2½-inch squares.

1 stick (½ cup) unsalted butter, cut into large pieces

6 ounces bittersweet chocolate, coarsely chopped (1 cup)

1½ cups sugar

3 large eggs

¼ cup unsweetened cocoa powder

½ teaspoon coarse salt

½ cup plus 2 tablespoons unbleached all-purpose flour

1 cup (6 ounces) milk chocolate chips

1 cup (6 ounces) white chocolate chips

1. Preheat oven to 350°F. Place six 4-inch shallow paper baking cups on a baking sheet. In a heatproof bowl set over (not in) a pot of simmering water, melt butter and bittersweet chocolate, stirring until smooth. Remove from heat and whisk in sugar. Whisk in eggs, one at a time, until combined. Whisk in cocoa powder and salt. Fold in flour until combined. Stir in both chocolate chips.

2. Fill cups three-quarters full with batter. Bake until set and a cake tester inserted into centers comes out with only a few moist crumbs attached, 30 to 35 minutes. Transfer to a wire rack and let cool completely. (Brownies can be stored in an airtight container at room temperature up to 3 days.)

TIP

For a nutty version, stir ½ cup chopped walnuts or pecans into the batter with the chocolate chips.

No-Bake Chocolate Truffles

MAKES 70

More candy than cookie, perhaps, but who is going to complain if a batch of these scrumptious bites turns up on a cookie tray? We're hooked on the little orbs of chocolate goodness. And they take no time to make—just whisk up some ganache, chill, and scoop. Finish by rolling the truffles in sprinkles, finely chopped nuts, or, as we did here, various unsweetened cocoa powders for a tone-on-tone display.

16 ounces dark or semisweet chocolate or a combination, finely chopped

1⅔ cups heavy cream

1 teaspoon vanilla extract

½ teaspoon coarse salt

Unsweetened cocoa powder, for rolling

1. Place chocolate in a medium heatproof bowl. In a small saucepan, bring cream to a simmer over medium-high heat; then immediately pour over chocolate. Cover bowl with plastic wrap pressed directly on the surface, and let stand 10 minutes. Uncover and whisk chocolate mixture until smooth. Mix in vanilla and salt. Pour into a 9-inch pie plate and let cool 15 minutes. Cover with plastic and refrigerate until completely set, about 3 hours.

2. With a melon baller, a 1-inch scoop, or a teaspoon, scoop out chocolate mixture and place on a piece of parchment. Coat hands with cocoa powder and roll truffles into balls; place on a parchment-lined baking sheet. Refrigerate until set, about 15 minutes. Roll in more cocoa powder just before serving or packing. (Truffles can be stored, covered with plastic and refrigerated, up to 2 weeks.)

TIP

To achieve an ombré effect, we rolled the truffles in different brands of unsweetened cocoa powders by color.

No-Bake Chocolate–Peanut Butter Cup Bars

MAKES SIXTEEN 2-INCH SQUARES

Think of this creamy no-bake candy bar as the classic peanut butter cup's more savvy, more fashionable sister. To achieve the swirly heart designs, just dot the chocolate surface with spoonfuls of peanut-butter mixture and drag a skewer or toothpick through them. (For a more abstract look, see Apricot Cheesecake Bars, on page 195.) To get the ultimate melt-in-your-mouth effect, use a smooth supermarket variety of peanut butter instead of a chunky or natural one.

Vegetable oil cooking spray

1 pound (1¾ cups) creamy peanut butter

1 stick (½ cup) plus 6 tablespoons unsalted butter, melted

1 teaspoon vanilla extract

2 cups confectioners' sugar, sifted

6 ounces semisweet or bittersweet chocolate, chopped

1. Coat bottom and sides of an 8-inch square baking pan with cooking spray. Line bottom and 2 sides with parchment, leaving a 2-inch overhang. In a large bowl, stir together 1½ cups peanut butter, 1 stick (½ cup) butter, and the vanilla until smooth. Stir in confectioners' sugar, ½ cup at a time, until smooth. Transfer to prepared pan; press with your hands to flatten and smooth top (if mixture is too sticky, dampen hands slightly).

2. Combine chocolate and 4 tablespoons butter in a heatproof bowl set over (not in) a pot of simmering water; stir with a rubber spatula until chocolate has melted and mixture is smooth. Remove bowl from heat and let cool slightly, stirring gently, about 3 minutes. Pour chocolate over peanut-butter mixture in baking pan, tilting pan to ensure chocolate spreads evenly across top.

3. In a small bowl, stir together remaining 2 tablespoons butter and remaining ¼ cup peanut butter until smooth. Let stand until slightly thickened, about 5 minutes. Drop ¼- to ¾-teaspoon rounds of mixture on top of chocolate in baking pan in 1-inch intervals. Drag the tip of a wooden skewer or toothpick quickly through center of each round to create a heart shape. Refrigerate until firm, at least 4 hours.

4. Run a paring knife along edges of pan on the 2 sides not lined with parchment. Lift cake from pan using parchment; cut into 2-inch bars. Serve cold. (Bars can be refrigerated in an airtight container up to 5 days.)

Salted Caramel Whoopie Pies

MAKES ABOUT 10

Sweet, spicy, and salty: This whoopie pie has it all. Cinnamon and allspice infuse the cake rounds, while a caramel-enriched buttercream claims the middle ground. A rim of pink rock salt brings it all together—enhancing and unifying the flavors while tempering the sweetness.

2½ cups unbleached all-purpose flour

2 teaspoons baking powder

¾ teaspoon coarse salt

1 teaspoon ground cinnamon

¼ teaspoon ground allspice

1 cup whole milk

1 teaspoon vanilla extract

5 tablespoons unsalted butter, room temperature

½ cup granulated sugar

½ cup packed light brown sugar

1 large egg, room temperature

Caramel Buttercream (page 245)

¾ teaspoon pink rock salt, such as Himalayan

2 tablespoons coarse sanding sugar

---

1. Preheat oven to 375°F. In a medium bowl, whisk together flour, baking powder, coarse salt, cinnamon, and allspice. In another medium bowl, combine milk and vanilla.

2. In a large bowl, with an electric mixer on high, beat butter with granulated and brown sugars until smooth, about 3 minutes. Add egg and beat until pale, about 2 minutes. With mixer on low, add flour mixture in 2 batches, alternating with milk mixture. Beat on medium-high until just combined, about 10 seconds. Transfer to a pastry bag fitted with a ⅝-inch round tip (such as Ateco #808).

3. Pipe 2½-inch-diameter mounds onto 3 parchment-lined baking sheets, spacing about 3 inches apart (no more than 8 per sheet). Bake, rotating sheets halfway through, until cookies spring back when lightly pressed, 12 to 14 minutes. Transfer sheets to wire racks and let cool completely.

4. Transfer buttercream to a pastry bag fitted with the ⅝-inch round tip. Pipe 2 tablespoons onto flat sides of half of cookies, then sandwich with remaining cookies. Refrigerate until firm, about 30 minutes.

5. In a small bowl, stir together rock salt and sanding sugar. Roll edges of sandwiches in sugar-salt mixture. (Whoopie pies can be refrigerated in airtight containers up to 3 days.)

Walnut-and-Honey Baklava

MAKES ABOUT 40 PIECES

The many buttered layers of phyllo dough, walnut filling, and sweet syrup make baklava the ultimate special-occasion dessert in Greece. Cutting it into a pretty pattern turns it into cookie-like bites. We used Greek honey in this recipe; it's dense, aromatic, and well worth seeking out. We use butter, too, but many Greek cooks use olive oil, which is a carryover from the days when butter was more of a precious (and therefore expensive) commodity.

4 cups walnut halves

1½ teaspoons ground cinnamon

1¾ cups sugar

½ cup honey, preferably Greek

2½ sticks (1¼ cups) unsalted butter, melted, plus more for brushing

28 sheets phyllo (from a 1½-pound package), thawed if frozen

1. Preheat oven to 375°F. In a food processor, pulse walnuts, cinnamon, and ½ cup sugar until finely ground.

2. In a saucepan over medium-high, bring 1 cup water and remaining 1¼ cups sugar to a boil. Immediately reduce to a simmer; cook until slightly thickened and sugar is dissolved, 3 to 5 minutes. Remove from heat and stir in honey. Let syrup cool completely.

3. Brush a 2-inch-deep, 12-inch round cake pan with butter. Trim each phyllo sheet into a 13-inch round (cover with plastic wrap and a damp towel as you work). Carefully layer 7 phyllo sheets in pan, brushing butter between each layer. (Since the edges dry out before the center, brush on butter from the edges inward.) Sprinkle one-third of nut mixture over top. Repeat process

twice more, brushing butter between each layer. Top with remaining 7 phyllo sheets, brushing butter between each layer.

4. Generously brush top layer with butter. Using a sharp knife with a very thin blade (such as a boning knife), cut baklava into quarters, cutting through all phyllo layers. Halve each quarter to create 8 equal wedges. Working within one wedge at a time, make 2 straight cuts, 1 inch apart, parallel to one side of wedge. Make 2 more cuts, parallel to opposite side of same wedge, creating a diamond pattern.

5. Bake until deep golden brown, 35 to 40 minutes. Remove from oven and pour syrup over baklava. Let cool completely before serving. (Baklava can be stored in an airtight container at room temperature up to 3 days or in the refrigerator up to 2 weeks.)

TIP

Make sure your hands are dry when working with phyllo. The dough will become gummy and unmanageable if it gets wet.

Brown-Butter Coconut-Cashew Blondies

MAKES ABOUT 1 DOZEN

Even if you're a brownie devotee, these bars might just convince you that blondes really do have more fun. They get their depth of flavor from nutty brown butter and brown sugar; cashews and coconut add dimension to the batter and a delightful, toasted crunch on top.

1¼ cups (2½ sticks) unsalted butter, plus more for pan

2¼ cups unbleached all-purpose flour, plus more for pan

2 cups packed light brown sugar

½ cup granulated sugar

3 large eggs

2½ teaspoons vanilla extract

1½ teaspoons baking powder

1½ teaspoons coarse salt

1 cup whole cashews, toasted (see page 248), plus ½ cup halved cashews

2 cups sweetened shredded coconut, toasted (see Tip)

½ cup unsweetened coconut flakes

1. Preheat oven to 350°F. Butter a 9-by-13-inch baking pan. Line bottom with parchment, leaving a 2-inch overhang on long sides. Butter and flour parchment.

2. In a small saucepan over medium-low heat, melt butter and cook, swirling pan occasionally, until golden brown and fragrant, about 8 minutes. Transfer to a large bowl; let cool. Add both sugars and stir until combined. Add eggs and vanilla;

beat to combine. Add flour, baking powder, salt, toasted cashews, and shredded coconut. Mix until thoroughly combined. Pour mixture into prepared pan, smoothing top with an offset spatula. Scatter cashew halves and coconut flakes evenly over top.

3. Bake until a cake tester inserted in the center just comes out clean, 35 to 40 minutes; tent with aluminum foil halfway through if topping is browning too quickly. Transfer to a wire rack and let cool. Lift blondies from pan using parchment; let cool completely on rack. Transfer to a cutting board and cut blondies into 3-inch squares. (Blondies can be stored in an airtight container at room temperature for up to 3 days.)

TIP

To toast coconut, spread in a single layer on a baking sheet and bake at 350°F, stirring halfway through, until golden, 9 to 10 minutes. Let cool completely.

Papillons

Living up to its namesake, the papillon (French for "butterfly") is shaped into ethereal "wings." Caramelized and tender, and made with just sugar and a multitude of flaky puff pastry (*pâte feuilletée*) layers, it is one of our favorite cookies. The puff pastry's butter content is key to the papillon's flavor, so it's best to avoid any pastry that is made with oil.

1 cup sugar, plus more for sprinkling and dipping

1 pound frozen puff pastry (preferably all butter), thawed

1. Sprinkle ½ cup sugar on a work surface. Place puff pastry on top of sugar and sprinkle evenly with remaining ½ cup sugar; press to adhere. Roll out to a 12-by-16-inch rectangle, approximately ⅛ inch thick.

2. Position pastry with a long side parallel to the edge of work surface. Fold each of the long sides of dough toward middle to meet without overlapping. Sprinkle lightly with about 2 tablespoons sugar. Fold one short side over to meet opposite short side. Sprinkle with about 1 tablespoon sugar. Finally, fold one long side in half to meet opposing long side. Coat with about 1 tablespoon sugar. Using your hands, press down firmly on dough; wrap tightly in plastic wrap and refrigerate at least 1 hour and preferably overnight.

3. Preheat oven to 450°F. Spritz 2 baking sheets with water. Place more sugar in a shallow bowl. Trim ends of chilled dough and slice crosswise into ¾-inch-thick slices. Dip cut sides of slices in sugar and transfer to baking sheets, spacing 3 inches apart.

4. Bake until sugar is caramelized and golden, 10 to 12 minutes. Using a wide spatula, carefully flip each cookie, rotate sheets, then return to oven and continue to bake until deep golden brown, about 6 minutes more. Transfer papillons to wire racks and let cool completely. Repeat with remaining slices. (Papillons are best eaten the day they are made, but can be stored between sheets of parchment in an airtight container at room temperature up to 3 days.)

TIP

Spraying water on the cookie sheet helps hold the puff pastry in place and keeps the cookies from sticking.

Apricot Cheesecake Bars

MAKES 2 DOZEN

Slightly tart apricot is an ideal foil for this creamy cheesecake. It also gives you the opportunity to try a painterly approach to baking. After adding dollops of fresh apricot compote to the cheesecake batter, use a chopstick, skewer, or the thin blade of a knife in shallow back-and-forth motions, figure eights, and loose spirals to make lovely decorative patterns.

18 graham crackers

1 cup plus 2 tablespoons sugar

Coarse salt

1 stick (½ cup) unsalted butter, melted

10 ounces fresh apricots (about 4), halved, pitted, and cut into eighths

1 tablespoon fresh lemon juice

2 packages (8 ounces each) cream cheese, room temperature

½ cup sour cream, room temperature

½ teaspoon vanilla extract

2 large eggs, room temperature, lightly beaten

1. Preheat oven to 350°F. In a food processor, process graham crackers, 2 tablespoons sugar, and ¼ teaspoon salt until fine crumbs form. Transfer to a medium bowl and stir in melted butter until crumbs are moistened. Wipe processor bowl clean. With a flat-bottomed 1-cup measure or glass, press the crumbs evenly into a 9-by-13-inch baking pan. Bake until crust is firm, about 15 minutes. Let cool on a wire rack. Reduce heat to 325°F.

2. In a small saucepan, bring apricots, ¼ cup sugar, and a pinch of salt to a boil over medium-high heat, stirring, until sugar dissolves. Reduce heat and simmer, stirring frequently, until mixture is shiny, about 10 minutes. In food processor, puree apricot mixture, lemon juice, and 1 tablespoon water.

3. In a large bowl, with an electric mixer on medium, beat cream cheese and sour cream until smooth. Add remaining ¾ cup sugar and beat until smooth. Add vanilla and a pinch of salt; beat to combine. Add eggs and beat until smooth, scraping down bowl as needed. Pour cream cheese mixture into crust and smooth top, using an offset spatula.

4. Randomly drop small spoonfuls of apricot puree onto cream cheese mixture. With a skewer or thin-bladed knife, gently swirl puree. Bake just until set, about 25 minutes. Transfer pan to a wire rack and let cool slightly, then refrigerate until chilled, about 2 hours. Cut into 24 squares. (Cheesecake bars can be refrigerated in an airtight container for up to 5 days.)

Whoopie Hearts

MAKES 2 DOZEN

These heartfelt whoopie pies are created with a simple V shape: Start by piping the chocolate batter into a three-inch diagonal line downward, then pipe another one to meet it. They bake up into billowy hearts, which we filled with a layer of raspberry-tinted Swiss meringue for just a little extra love.

¾ cup frozen raspberries

3½ cups unbleached all-purpose flour

1 teaspoon coarse salt

1½ cups unsweetened cocoa powder

1 teaspoon baking soda

1 teaspoon baking powder

2 sticks (1 cup) unsalted butter, room temperature

2 cups sugar

2 large eggs, room temperature

2 teaspoons vanilla extract

2 cups buttermilk, room temperature

Swiss Meringue Filling (page 246)

1. Preheat oven to 400°F. Thaw raspberries in a sieve set over a bowl; press to extract ¼ cup juice. Reserve juice for Swiss meringue filling (discard fruit).

2. In a medium bowl, whisk together flour, salt, cocoa powder, baking soda, and baking powder. In a large bowl, with an electric mixer on medium, beat butter and sugar until pale and fluffy, about 3 minutes. Add eggs and vanilla. Beat until well combined. Add flour mixture in 2 additions, alternating with buttermilk. Mix until combined.

3. To create heart shapes, form the letter V: Transfer batter to a pastry bag fitted with a ½-inch round tip (such as Ateco #806). Pipe a 3-inch diagonal line downward, onto a parchment-lined baking sheet. Pipe another one to meet it. (The tops are about 3 inches wide; see page 242 for piping directions.) Bake until cookies spring back when lightly touched with finger, about 12 minutes. Transfer to a wire rack to cool. Repeat with remaining batter.

4. Assemble whoopie pies: Add reserved raspberry juice to Swiss meringue filling and stir to combine. Transfer filling to another pastry bag fitted with a ½-inch round tip. Pipe filling onto flat sides of half the cookies, then sandwich with remaining cookies. (Whoopie pies can be refrigerated in an airtight container up to 3 days.)

TIP

Keep the pastry bag stable while filling it by placing it inside a tall container.

Fudgy

Chewy

Cakey

PERFECTING
BROWNIES

Everyone loves brownies, but some like these chocolatey squares rich and dense, while others prefer a chewy center, and still others favor a lighter, cakey crumb. How does a baker get it just right? Fudgy brownies have a higher fat-to-flour ratio than cakey ones, so add more fat—in this case, butter and chocolate. A cakey batch has more flour and relies on baking powder for leavening. And adding a bit of oil along with butter in the batter results in a brownie with an addictively chewy texture. See the recipes that follow to get an idea of the ratios needed to achieve your ideal brownie.

Cakey Brownies

MAKES NINE 3-INCH SQUARES

4 tablespoons unsalted butter, cut into large pieces, plus more for pan

4 ounces bitter-sweet chocolate, coarsely chopped

1½ cups sugar

3 large eggs

¼ cup unsweetened Dutch-process cocoa powder

½ teaspoon coarse salt

1½ cups unbleached all-purpose flour

¾ teaspoon baking powder

1. Preheat oven to 350°F. Butter a 9-inch square baking pan. Line with parchment, leaving a slight overhang on 2 sides; butter parchment.

2. In a medium heatproof bowl set over (not in) a pot of simmering water, melt butter and chocolate, stirring until smooth. Remove from heat and whisk in sugar. Whisk in eggs, one at a time, until combined. Whisk in cocoa powder and salt. Fold in flour and baking powder until combined. Pour batter into prepared pan, smoothing top with spatula.

3. Bake until set and a cake tester inserted into the center comes out with moist crumbs, about 30 minutes. Transfer pan to a wire rack and let cool, about 15 minutes. Lift brownies from pan using parchment; remove parchment. Transfer brownies to wire rack and let cool completely. Cut into 9 squares. (Brownies can be stored in an airtight container at room temperature up to 2 days.)

Fudgy Brownies

MAKES NINE 3-INCH SQUARES

1 stick (½ cup) unsalted butter, cut into large pieces, plus more for pan

6 ounces bittersweet chocolate, chopped

1½ cups sugar

3 large eggs

¼ cup unsweetened Dutch-process cocoa powder

½ teaspoon coarse salt

½ cup plus 2 tablespoons unbleached all-purpose flour

1. Preheat oven to 350°F. Butter a 9-inch square baking pan. Line with parchment, leaving a slight overhang on 2 sides; butter parchment.

2. In a medium heatproof bowl set over (not in) a pot of simmering water, melt butter and chocolate, stirring until smooth. Remove from heat and whisk in sugar. Whisk in eggs, one at a time, until combined. Whisk in cocoa and salt. Fold in flour until combined. Pour batter into prepared pan, smoothing top with spatula.

3. Bake until set and a cake tester inserted into the center comes out with moist crumbs, 35 to 40 minutes. Transfer pan to a wire rack and let cool slightly, about 15 minutes. Lift brownies from pan using parchment; remove parchment. Transfer brownies to wire rack and let cool completely. Cut into 9 squares. (Brownies can be stored in an airtight container at room temperature up to 2 days.)

Tips for Brownies

● Don't scrimp on the chocolate—it's the core flavor in brownies. Choose the best quality you can find, such as Valrhona or Guittard with at least 61% cacao in bittersweet.

● To achieve a shiny, crackled top crust, whisk the eggs into the batter until glossy.

● Scraping down the sides of the bowl when adding the flour prevents white flour pockets or streaks.

● Add toasted nuts, such as walnuts or pecans, or chocolate chunks to the batter just after incorporating the flour.

● Butter the parchment. You can "flour" it with Dutch-process cocoa powder, which gives a nice chocolate flavor to the brownies' edges.

● Use small metal binder clips to fasten the parchment paper to the sides of the pan. This allows you to more easily pour in the brownie mixture, and, if you're using a convection oven, it will prevent the parchment from blowing around as air circulates while baking.

● Sprinkle flaky salt, such as Maldon, on top of the batter just before baking for a truly sweet-and-salty treat.

● Let the brownies cool completely before removing from the pan and cutting into squares. (Don't cut the brownies in the pan to avoid scratching its bottom.)

Chewy Brownies

MAKES SIXTEEN 2¼-INCH SQUARES

7 tablespoons unsalted butter, room temperature, plus more for pan	7 ounces unsweetened chocolate, finely chopped
¾ cup plus 2 tablespoons unbleached all-purpose flour	3 tablespoons safflower or coconut oil
¼ teaspoon baking powder	1 cup granulated sugar
½ teaspoon coarse salt	1 cup packed light brown sugar
	3 large eggs, room temperature

1. Preheat oven to 350°F. Butter a 9-inch square baking pan. Line with parchment, leaving a slight overhang on 2 sides; butter parchment.

2. In a medium bowl, whisk together flour, baking powder, and salt. In a medium heatproof bowl set over (not in) a pot of simmering water, melt chocolate and butter with oil. Remove from heat. Add both sugars and whisk 10 seconds. Add eggs and whisk vigorously until glossy and smooth, 45 seconds. Using a rubber spatula, stir in dry ingredients. Pour batter evenly into prepared pan, smoothing top with spatula.

3. Bake until set and a cake tester inserted into the center comes out with moist crumbs, 35 to 40 minutes. Transfer pan to a wire rack and let cool, about 15 minutes. Lift brownies from pan using parchment; remove parchment. Transfer brownies to wire rack and let cool completely. Cut into 16 squares. (Brownies can be stored in an airtight container at room temperature up to 2 days.)

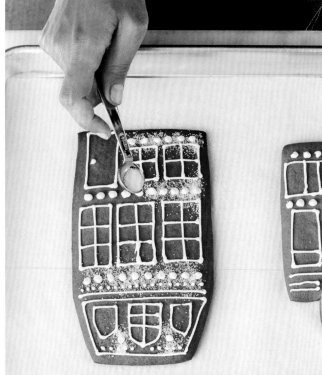
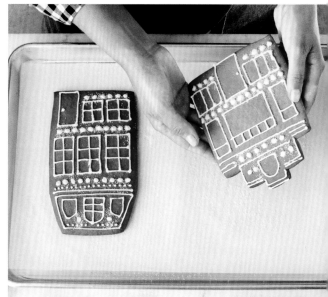

7

CELEBRATION COOKIES

Get caught in a Halloween spider's web,
wear your heart on your sleeve for
Valentine's Day, set off some fireworks
for the Fourth of July—the most special days
call for the most festive cookies.

Honey-Spice Gingerbread Townhouses

MAKES 1 DOZEN

A fragrant gingerbread cookie is the basis for these elegant and impressive townhouses. The dough is sweetened with honey and spiced with warm ginger, cinnamon, nutmeg, and cloves. Since the flavor of gingerbread cookies improves over time, these can be displayed during the holidays and are perfect for gifting. When decorating the townhouses, remember to squeeze the pastry bag with one hand and use the other hand to guide the tip.

5½ cups unbleached all-purpose flour, plus more for dusting

1½ teaspoons coarse salt

1 teaspoon baking soda

4 teaspoons ground ginger

1 teaspoon ground cinnamon

1 teaspoon freshly grated nutmeg

½ teaspoon ground cloves

2 sticks (1 cup) unsalted butter, room temperature

1 cup granulated sugar

2 large eggs

1 cup honey

½ cup unsulfured molasses

Royal Icing (page 244)

Fine sanding sugar, for decorating

1. In a large bowl, whisk together flour, salt, baking soda, and spices. In another large bowl, with an electric mixer on medium-high, beat butter and granulated sugar until pale and fluffy, about 3 minutes. Beat in eggs, one at a time, then honey and molasses. With mixer on low, gradually add flour mixture until well combined. Divide dough into 3 pieces, wrap each in plastic wrap, and refrigerate until firm but still pliable, about 1 hour.

2. Preheat oven to 350°F. Working with a third of dough at a time, roll out to ¼-inch thickness on generously floured parchment. Brush off excess flour, transfer dough on parchment to a baking sheet, and freeze until firm, about 15 minutes.

3. Use the townhouse templates (page 247) or 6-inch-tall house-shaped cutters to cut out 12 cookies. Transfer houses to parchment-lined baking sheets. Freeze until firm, about 15 minutes. Bake cookies 6 minutes. Remove sheets from oven and tap firmly on counter to flatten cookies. Return to oven, rotating sheets, and bake until cookies are crisp but not darkened, 6 to 8 minutes more. Transfer sheets to wire racks and let cool completely.

4. Transfer icing to a pastry bag fitted with a fine plain tip (such as Ateco #1) or a closed star tip (such as Ateco #13). Pipe designs on cookies, then immediately sprinkle with sanding sugar; tap off excess. Let cookies stand at room temperature until set, at least 2 hours, and preferably overnight. (Cookies can be stored in an airtight container at room temperature up to 1 week.)

Glazed Spiced Snowflakes

MAKES 7 LARGE, 12 MEDIUM, AND 36 SMALL COOKIES

The intricate pattern on these snowflake cookies—whose spiced flavor
is inspired by Speculaas—comes from an unexpected source: crocheted doilies.
The design is imprinted by placing a doily on top of the rolled-out dough
and then using a rolling pin to transfer it (see page 238). The thicker the doily,
the clearer the imprint (thin paper ones won't do the trick).

FOR THE COOKIES

3½ cups unbleached all-purpose flour, plus more for dusting

½ teaspoon baking soda

½ teaspoon coarse salt

1 teaspoon ground cinnamon

1 teaspoon ground ginger

½ teaspoon ground cardamom

¼ teaspoon ground coriander

⅛ teaspoon ground cloves

1½ sticks (¾ cup) unsalted butter, room temperature

1 cup packed dark brown sugar

FOR THE GLAZE

1½ cups confectioners' sugar, sifted

¼ cup whole milk, plus more if needed

⅛ teaspoon vanilla extract

1. Make the cookies: In a large bowl, whisk together flour, baking soda, salt, and spices. In another large bowl, with an electric mixer on medium-high, beat butter with brown sugar until pale and fluffy, about 3 minutes. Add half the flour mixture, then ⅓ cup water, then remaining flour mixture, beating on low after each addition until just incorporated. Shape dough into 3 disks and wrap in plastic. Refrigerate until firm, at least 1 hour and up to overnight.

2. Working with one disk at a time, roll out to ¼-inch thickness on lightly floured parchment. Cover with a doily and gently roll to make an imprint. (Dough should now be about ⅛ inch thick.) Remove doily and freeze dough until firm, about 15 minutes.

3. Using a 5-inch snowflake-shaped cutter, cut snowflakes from one disk. Cut remaining dough disks using 3-inch and 1½-inch snowflake-shaped cutters. Chill and reroll scraps. Arrange large cookies on a parchment-lined baking sheet and medium and small cookies together on another; freeze until firm, about 15 minutes.

4. Meanwhile, preheat oven to 325°F. Bake, rotating sheets halfway through, until cookies are set around edges, 16 to 18 minutes for large, 12 to 14 minutes for medium and small. Transfer sheets to wire racks and let cool completely.

5. Make the glaze: In a medium bowl, whisk together confectioners' sugar, milk, and vanilla until smooth. If necessary, add more milk, ½ teaspoon at a time, until glaze is slightly thicker than cream. Dip each cookie, imprint side down, into glaze, tilting to evenly coat. Transfer to rack until glaze is set, about 10 minutes. (Cookies can be stored in an airtight container at room temperature up to 3 days.)

Double-Chocolate Peppermint Cookies

MAKES ABOUT 2 DOZEN

To make this irresistible hybrid of chocolate cookie sandwich and peppermint bark, you will need two sizes of fluted cookie cutters. The larger shapes the cookie "frame" and the smaller creates the "window" to hold tiny peppermint candy pieces.

¾ cup unbleached all-purpose flour, plus more for dusting

⅓ cup unsweetened Dutch-process cocoa powder

⅛ teaspoon coarse salt

6 tablespoons unsalted butter, room temperature

¾ cup confectioners' sugar, sifted

1 large egg, room temperature

½ teaspoon vanilla extract

4 ounces milk chocolate, finely chopped

½ cup heavy cream

½ teaspoon peppermint extract

¼ cup peppermint candies, coarsely chopped or crushed

1. In a medium bowl, whisk flour, cocoa, and salt. In a large bowl, with an electric mixer on medium-high, beat butter with sugar until pale and fluffy, about 2 minutes. Beat in egg and vanilla. Gradually add flour mixture and mix on low to combine. Divide dough in half, shape into disks, and wrap each in plastic. Refrigerate until firm, about 1 hour.

2. Preheat oven to 325°F. Working with one disk at a time (keeping the other refrigerated), roll out on lightly floured parchment to a scant ⅛-inch thickness. Cut out about 50 rounds with a 1¾-inch fluted round cutter. Chill and reroll scraps (if dough becomes too soft, freeze 15 minutes). Use a ½-inch fluted round

cutter to cut out centers of half the rounds. Arrange rounds on parchment-lined baking sheets, about 1 inch apart. Freeze until firm, 15 minutes. Brush off excess flour with a pastry brush.

3. Bake, rotating sheets halfway through, until edges of cookies are firm, 13 to 15 minutes. Transfer sheets to wire racks and let cool completely. (You can bake the small, plain cutout rounds separately for 6 to 8 minutes.)

4. Place chocolate in a heatproof bowl. Heat cream in a small saucepan over medium-high until just bubbling around edges. Remove from heat and stir in peppermint extract. Pour mixture over chocolate; let stand 10 minutes, then stir until smooth. Let stand, stirring occasionally, until firm enough to spread, about 30 minutes.

5. Spread 1 teaspoon filling on each uncut cookie; top with cut cookies. Sprinkle chopped candies in window of each top cookie. Refrigerate until set, about 20 minutes. (Assembled cookies can be refrigerated in an airtight container up to 2 days.)

Gingerbread Trees

MAKES 2 DOZEN

These festive snow-tipped Christmas trees will bring color and spiced warmth to your batch of holiday cookies. We chose a fragrant gingerbread base, so the trunk would be true to form, but a vanilla sugar dough works just as beautifully. Feel free to play around with sizes if you have different tree cookie cutters—just remember to put like-sized trees on the same sheet, as the smaller ones will need less time in the oven.

6 cups unbleached all-purpose flour, plus more for dusting

1 teaspoon baking soda

½ teaspoon baking powder

2 sticks (1 cup) unsalted butter, room temperature

1 cup packed dark-brown sugar

4 teaspoons ground ginger

4 teaspoons ground cinnamon

1½ teaspoons ground cloves

1 teaspoon finely ground pepper

1½ teaspoons coarse salt

2 large eggs, room temperature

1 cup unsulfured molasses

Royal Icing (page 244)

Green gel-paste food coloring

1. In a large bowl, whisk together flour, baking soda, and baking powder. In another large bowl, with an electric mixer on medium-high, beat butter and sugar until pale and fluffy, 2 to 3 minutes. Mix in ginger, cinnamon, cloves, pepper, and salt. Beat in eggs, one at a time, then molasses. Gradually add flour mixture and mix on low until just combined. Divide dough into 3 pieces; wrap each in plastic. Refrigerate until chilled, at least 1 hour.

2. Preheat oven to 350°F. On a lightly floured surface, roll out dough to ⅛ inch thick. Cut out Christmas tree shapes and transfer to parchment-lined baking sheets. Bake cookies, rotating sheets halfway through, until crisp but not darkened, about 20 minutes. Transfer sheets to wire racks and let cool completely.

3. To decorate cookies: Tint three-quarters royal icing with green gel-paste food coloring. Transfer icing to a pastry bag fitted with a small round tip (Ateco #1 or #2). Flood cookies with icing (see page 243), leaving tree trunk bare. Let set at room temperature, at least 12 hours and up to overnight.

4. Place remaining white royal icing in a pastry bag fitted with a small round tip and pipe lines of snow onto branches. Let set at room temperature, about 4 hours. (Cookies can be stored in an airtight container at room temperature up to 3 days.)

Candy Cane Cookies

MAKES ABOUT 2 DOZEN

Give the candy cane a fanciful twist (literally) by making it a supersized sugar cookie, two-toned and glittering with sanding sugar. It even tastes like the original candy, due to the addition of peppermint extract.

2 sticks (1 cup) unsalted butter, room temperature

1 cup granulated sugar

1 large egg, room temperature

½ teaspoon vanilla extract

½ teaspoon peppermint extract

¼ teaspoon coarse salt

2½ cups unbleached all-purpose flour, plus more for dusting

Red gel-paste food coloring

1 large egg white, beaten

Coarse sanding sugar, for decorating

1. In a large bowl, with an electric mixer on medium, beat butter and granulated sugar until pale and fluffy, about 2 minutes. Beat in egg, both extracts, and salt. Gradually add flour and mix on low until just combined. Divide dough in half. Knead food coloring into one half until desired color is reached. Form dough into disks, wrap each in plastic, and refrigerate 20 minutes and up to overnight. (Dough can be frozen up to 1 month; thaw in the refrigerator before using.)

2. Divide untinted dough into 12 pieces. On a lightly floured surface, shape each into a 12-inch-long log. Refrigerate until firm but pliable, about 10 minutes. Repeat with tinted dough. Twist a tinted and an untinted piece together; roll gently to form a log. Cut crosswise into 2 equal pieces; bend one end to form a cane. Repeat. Arrange on parchment-lined sheets, about 2 inches apart. Cover with plastic wrap and chill 1 hour and up to overnight.

3. Preheat oven to 325°F. Bake, rotating sheets halfway through, until cookies are firm but not taking on any color, 20 to 24 minutes. Transfer sheets to wire racks and let cool completely.

4. Brush each candy cane with egg white and sprinkle with sanding sugar; tap off excess. (Cookies can be stored in an airtight container at room temperature up to 1 week.)

TIP

You might want to don a pair of gloves when kneading food coloring into the dough, to avoid staining your hands.

Fruitcake Cookies

MAKES 4 DOZEN

Want to up the appeal of the iconic holiday cake? Try turning it into an enticing batch of bite-sized cookies. Like traditional fruitcake, these delights are studded with high-quality dried fruit—glacé cherries, dried papaya, and candied citron—but the delicate portion size, delicious coating of chocolate fondant, and edible gold leaf take them to the next level.

2 sticks (1 cup) unsalted butter, room temperature, plus more for pan

2 cups unbleached all-purpose flour

½ teaspoon ground cinnamon

½ teaspoon coarse salt

⅛ teaspoon ground cardamom

¼ teaspoon baking powder

7 ounces almond paste (1 tube), cut into small pieces

1 cup sugar

2 large eggs, room temperature

¼ cup kirsch or brandy

1 pound (3 cups) mixed candied and dried fruit, such as glacé cherries, dried papaya, and candied citron, cut into ½-inch pieces

Poured Chocolate Fondant (page 244)

Edible gold leaf, for decorating (optional)

1. Preheat oven to 325°F. Butter a 9-by-13-inch baking sheet and line with parchment, leaving a 2-inch overhang on long sides. Butter parchment. In a medium bowl, whisk together flour, cinnamon, salt, cardamom, and baking powder.

2. Pulse almond paste in a food processor until crumbly; add sugar and pulse just to combine. Transfer mixture to a large bowl. Add butter and, with an electric mixer on medium-high, beat until pale and fluffy, scraping down sides of bowl, about 2 minutes. Add eggs, one at a time,

beating well after each addition. Beat in 2 tablespoons kirsch. Gradually add flour mixture, beating on low, until fully combined. Beat in fruit.

3. Scrape batter into prepared sheet, smoothing top with an offset spatula. Bake until pale golden, about 1 hour, 15 minutes. Brush with remaining 2 tablespoons kirsch. Transfer sheet to a wire rack and let cool 45 minutes. Use parchment overhang to lift out of pan; let cool completely on rack. Refrigerate at least 4 hours and preferably overnight. Using a sharp knife, trim edges and cut into 1¼-inch squares.

4. Working in batches (keeping the rest refrigerated), place one cookie on a fork. Spoon fondant over top, allowing it to coat entire cookie and excess to drip back into bowl. Place on a wire rack set over a baking sheet. If at any time fondant gets too thick, add hot water, 1 tablespoon at a time, and warm in the microwave or over a pot of simmering water. Let cookies stand until set, about 30 minutes. If desired, decorate with a few flecks of edible gold leaf. (Cookies can be refrigerated in an airtight container up to 5 days.)

Pfeffernüsse

MAKES ABOUT 5 DOZEN

German for "pepper nut," *pfeffernüsse* cookies are traditional holiday treats, named for their nutlike size and for the pinch of pepper added to the dough before baking. Black pepper joins a quartet of warm spices—cinnamon, nutmeg, allspice, and cloves. We gave our glazed version an extra shot of depth, sprinkling the sweets with ground pink peppercorns to finish.

FOR THE COOKIES

2¼ cups unbleached all-purpose flour

¼ teaspoon baking soda

¾ teaspoon ground cinnamon

½ teaspoon ground allspice

¼ teaspoon ground cloves

¼ teaspoon freshly grated nutmeg

¼ teaspoon freshly ground black pepper

1 stick (½ cup) unsalted butter, room temperature

¾ cup packed light brown sugar

¼ cup unsulfured molasses

1 large egg

½ teaspoon vanilla extract

FOR THE GLAZE

3½ cups confectioners' sugar, sifted

⅓ cup whole milk, plus more if needed

¼ teaspoon kirsch or other cherry-flavored liqueur (optional)

TO DECORATE

Coarsely ground pink peppercorns

1. Make the cookies: Preheat oven to 350°F. In a medium bowl, whisk together flour, baking soda, and spices. In a large bowl, with an electric mixer on medium, beat butter, brown sugar, and molasses until fluffy, about 3 minutes. Beat in egg and vanilla until combined. Gradually add flour mixture and mix on low until just combined. (Dough will be dry and crumbly.)

2. Pinch off a heaping teaspoon of dough and, with wet hands, roll into a ball; transfer to parchment-lined baking sheet. Repeat process with remaining dough, spacing balls 1½ inches apart. (Dough can be frozen at this point, covered tightly with plastic wrap, up to 1 month.)

3. Working in batches, bake cookies, rotating sheets halfway through, until golden and firm to the touch with slight cracking, about 15 minutes. Transfer sheets to wire racks to cool completely.

4. Make the glaze: Fit a baking sheet with a wire rack. In a medium bowl, whisk together confectioners' sugar, milk, and kirsch, if using. Using a fork, dip each cookie in glaze to coat. Tap to remove excess glaze and place on wire rack to dry. Repeat with remaining cookies.

5. Decorate: While the glaze is still wet, top cookies with a pinch of peppercorns. Let glaze dry completely before serving. (Cookies can be stored in an airtight container at room temperature up to 2 weeks.)

Stained-Glass Sugar Cookies

MAKES ABOUT 1 DOZEN

Crushed hard candy can be tucked into sugar-cookie cutouts to produce a colorful stained-glass effect. For easy cleanup, sort candy by color and place in individual zip-top plastic bags. Cover the bags with a kitchen towel and use a rolling pin to crush (not pulverize) the candy.

3 cups unbleached all-purpose flour, plus more for dusting

¾ teaspoon baking powder

¼ teaspoon fine salt

2 sticks (1 cup) unsalted butter, room temperature

1¼ cups sugar

4 large egg yolks

1 tablespoon vanilla extract

1 cup very finely crushed hard candy, such as Jolly Rancher, in various colors, colors kept separate

1. In a medium bowl, whisk together flour, baking powder, and salt. In a large bowl, with an electric mixer on medium-high, beat butter and sugar until pale and fluffy, about 3 minutes. Add egg yolks and vanilla and beat to combine. Gradually add flour mixture and mix on low until just combined. Shape dough into 2 disks, wrap in plastic, and refrigerate 30 minutes.

2. Working with one disk at a time, roll out dough between floured parchment to ⅛-inch thickness. Stack dough in parchment on a baking sheet and refrigerate until firm, about 30 minutes.

3. Preheat oven to 350°F. With a 4-inch ornament-shaped cutter, cut out dough. Place cookies on 2 parchment-lined baking sheets, spacing about 2 inches apart. Using aspic cutters, cut out desired designs. Using a chopstick, punch a hole near the top for hanging, if desired. Freeze until firm, about 15 minutes.

4. Bake, rotating sheets halfway through, until cookies are pale but set, about 14 minutes. Remove sheets from oven; fill cutouts with crushed candy. Continue to bake until cookies begin to brown at edges and candy is just melted, 1 to 2 minutes more. Transfer sheets to wire racks and let cool completely. (Cookies can be stored in an airtight container at room temperature up to 1 week.)

TIP

We used aspic cutters to form the interior shapes. If you don't have any, you can use other kitchen tools for similar effects, such as an apple corer, a small biscuit cutter, or a large straw. Bake until the candy is just melted; otherwise it will begin to bubble.

Snowball Truffles

MAKES 2 DOZEN

Creamy white chocolate and flaky coconut make these festive truffles look like miniature snowballs. Technically these darling confections aren't cookies, but with only five ingredients and a virtually effortless assembly, we couldn't resist them.

½ cup unsalted cashews, toasted (see page 248)

½ cup unsweetened shredded coconut, plus more for rolling

7 ounces white chocolate, coarsely chopped, plus more, melted (see page 248), for rolling

½ cup heavy cream

Pinch of coarse salt

1. In a food processor, pulse cashews and coconut until finely ground. Add chocolate and pulse just to combine.

2. In a small saucepan over medium-low, heat cream with a pinch of salt until simmering. Pour hot cream mixture into food processor; pulse until well combined and chocolate is melted. Transfer mixture to a shallow bowl and refrigerate until set, at least 1 hour and up to 2 days.

3. Scoop chilled mixture, 2 teaspoons at a time (use a 1⅜-inch or other small scoop), onto parchment-lined baking sheets. Roll into balls. Refrigerate until chilled, about 30 minutes.

4. Place more coconut in a shallow dish. Place some melted chocolate in the palm of your hand; roll a truffle in the melted chocolate to generously coat, then roll in coconut, pressing gently to adhere. Repeat with remaining balls. Refrigerate 1 hour, then transfer to an airtight container, stacking truffles no more than 2 or 3 high, and refrigerate. Bring to room temperature just before serving. (Truffles can be refrigerated up to 2 weeks.)

TIP

Use a high-quality white chocolate, such as Callebaut or Valrhona. Cocoa butter, not cacao solids, gives white chocolate its rich, creamy flavor, along with milk, sugar, vanilla, and lecithin.

Easter Chick Cookies

MAKES 3 DOZEN

Chicks and eggs are sure signs of spring—and both look sweet nestled in baskets or displayed on the dessert table at brunch. Ours are iced lemon shortbread and are simply decorated with sanding sugar, sprinkles, mini chocolate chips, and candy—so it's easy for little ones to help.

FOR THE COOKIES

2 cups unbleached all-purpose flour

¾ teaspoon coarse salt

2 sticks (1 cup) unsalted butter, room temperature

½ cup confectioners' sugar, sifted

1 teaspoon vanilla extract

FOR THE ICING

3 cups confectioners' sugar, sifted

6 tablespoons fresh lemon juice (from 2 lemons)

Yellow fine sanding sugar, jumbo candy sequins, orange and yellow sprinkles, candy hearts, and mini chocolate chips, for decorating

1. Make the cookies: In a small bowl, whisk together flour and salt. In a large bowl, with an electric mixer on medium-high, beat butter until fluffy, 3 to 5 minutes. Add confectioners' sugar, and continue to beat until pale and fluffy, occasionally scraping down sides of bowl, about 2 minutes more. Beat in vanilla. Gradually add flour mixture, and mix on low, scraping sides if necessary, until flour is just incorporated and dough sticks together when squeezed with fingers.

2. Shape dough into 2 disks and wrap each in plastic. Refrigerate until firm, at least 1 hour.

3. Preheat oven to 325°F. Roll out one disk to ¼-inch thickness; cut out shapes with 2½-inch-tall egg cookie cutter. (Or use a 2½-inch-tall oval cookie cutter, and pinch one end to create an egg shape.) Transfer cookies to parchment-lined baking sheets, spacing about 1 inch apart. Reroll scraps and repeat. Repeat with remaining disk.

4. Bake until firm and golden, 13 to 15 minutes. For flatter cookies, tap sheets on counter halfway through baking and again afterward. Let cool completely on wire racks.

5. Make the icing: In a medium bowl, stir together confectioners' sugar and lemon juice. Transfer icing to a pastry bag fitted with a small round tip (such as Ateco #1 or #2). Flood cookies with icing (see page 243).

6. For the chicks: Dip an iced cookie in sanding sugar; let dry. Dot candy sequins with icing; overlap to create feathers. Use orange sprinkles for feet, a candy heart for a beak, and upside-down mini chocolate chips for eyes.

7. For the eggs: Lay orange or yellow sprinkles in a zigzag pattern halfway up an iced cookie. Sprinkle bottom with sanding sugar. (Cookies can be stored in an airtight container at room temperature up to 5 days.)

Bunny Cookies

MAKES ABOUT 3 DOZEN

These bite-sized sugar cookies are the minimalist's Easter bunny—each starts with an oblong ball of dough and takes shape with just two quick snips and a couple of pokes with a toothpick. They're as simple as can be, and will look adorable snuggled into a basket or peering over the edge of a breakfast plate.

2 sticks (1 cup) unsalted butter, room temperature

¾ cup sugar

1 teaspoon vanilla extract

½ teaspoon coarse salt

1 large egg white

Gel-paste food coloring in pink and lavender

3 cups unbleached all-purpose flour

1. In a large bowl, with an electric mixer on medium, beat butter and sugar until pale and fluffy, about 2 minutes. Beat in vanilla, salt, and egg white. For pink bunnies, add 1 to 2 drops of gel for desired color; for lavender bunnies, add 1 to 2 drops. Gradually add flour and mix on low until combined.

2. For each bunny, roll 1 tablespoon dough between palms to create a 1-inch oval. Hold kitchen shears at a 30-degree angle; snip ears about ½ inch from front. (Do not cut all the way through.)

3. With a toothpick, poke holes for eyes. Transfer to parchment-lined baking sheets. Refrigerate until firm, about 1 hour.

4. Preheat oven to 350°F. Bake cookies, rotating sheets halfway through, just until golden brown on bottoms, 22 to 25 minutes. Transfer to wire racks and let cool completely. (Cookies can be stored in an airtight container at room temperature up to 3 days.)

TIP

Use your sharpest, finest shears to snip the ears (not large, thick kitchen shears).

Easter Egg Puzzle Cookies

MAKES ABOUT 3 DOZEN

You know what they say—you can't make Easter cookies without breaking a few eggs. We took that idea to heart in creating these clever puzzle cookies. All you need to do is cut oval shapes out of sugar-cookie dough, "break" them into pieces after baking, and finish with pastel royal icing and sanding sugar. The most fun comes post-hunt, when it's time to put them back together again.

4 cups all-purpose unbleached flour, plus more for dusting

1 teaspoon baking powder

½ teaspoon coarse salt

2 sticks (1 cup) unsalted butter, room temperature

2 cups granulated sugar

2 large eggs

2 teaspoons vanilla extract

Royal Icing (page 244)

Gel-paste food coloring in violet and soft pink

Sanding sugar, for sprinkling (optional)

1. In a large bowl, whisk together flour, baking powder, and salt. In another bowl, with an electric mixer on medium, beat butter and granulated sugar until pale and fluffy, about 3 minutes. Beat in eggs, one at a time. Gradually add flour mixture and mix on low until combined. Add vanilla. Wrap dough in plastic and refrigerate for 1 hour.

2. Roll out dough to ⅛-inch thickness on a lightly floured surface. Cut out egg shapes with a 2½-inch oval cutter; pinch one end to create an egg shape. Transfer cookies to parchment-lined baking sheets, spacing about 1 inch apart. Refrigerate until firm, about 30 minutes. (At this point, dough can be refrigerated up to 2 days or frozen up to 5 days.)

3. Preheat oven to 325°F. Bake cookies until edges are golden, 8 to 10 minutes. Immediately cut cookies into puzzle pieces using a paring knife. Transfer to wire racks and let cool completely.

4. Divide icing into batches, and mix in a different shade of food coloring to each to tint. Arrange cookie pieces together, and flood cookies with icing (see page 243). Sprinkle with sanding sugar, if desired. Let icing dry completely before piping dots and stripes. (Iced cookies can be stored in an airtight container at room temperature up to 3 days.)

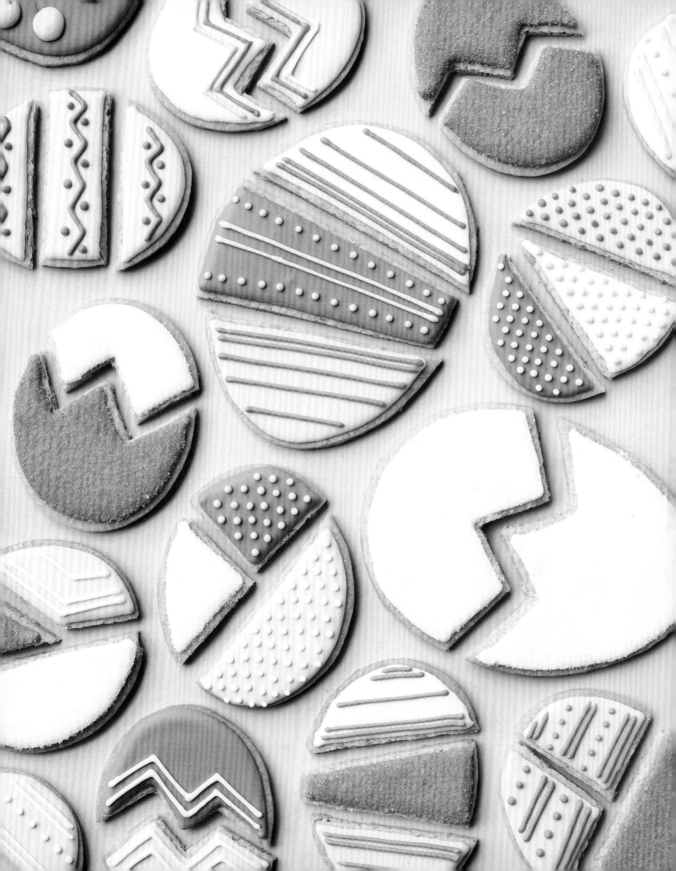

Fireworks Cookies

MAKES ABOUT 7 DOZEN 1³/₄-INCH COOKIES, 5 DOZEN 2¹/₄-INCH COOKIES, THIRTY 2³/₄-INCH COOKIES, OR THIRTEEN 3¹/₂-INCH COOKIES

Put on a dazzling Fourth of July show with a display of these patriotic beauties. The decorative lines of the fireworks look a lot trickier to make than they are; all you need is a toothpick to swirl together the white and colored royal icing. We used sugar cookies, but any flat cookie will work.

4 cups unbleached all-purpose flour, plus more for dusting

1 teaspoon baking powder

Coarse salt

2 sticks (1 cup) unsalted butter, room temperature

2 cups sugar

2 large eggs

2 teaspoons vanilla extract

Royal Icing (page 244)

Gel-paste food coloring in red, royal blue, and navy blue

1. Sift flour, baking powder, and ½ teaspoon salt into a large bowl. In another bowl, with an electric mixer on medium-high, beat butter and sugar until pale and fluffy, about 3 minutes. Beat in eggs, one at a time. With mixer on low, gradually add flour mixture, then vanilla. Shape dough into 2 disks, wrap in plastic, and refrigerate for at least 1 hour and up to 5 days. (It can also be frozen up to 1 month and thawed in refrigerator. Let sit at room temperature until soft enough to roll.)

2. Preheat oven to 325°F. Roll out dough to ¼-inch thickness on a floured surface. Cut out cookies using a 1¾-, 2¼-, 2¾-, or 3½-inch round cookie cutter, rerolling scraps once. Transfer to parchment-lined baking sheets. Refrigerate until firm, about 30 minutes.

3. Bake cookies until edges just start to brown, 17 to 19 minutes. Transfer cookies to wire racks and let cool.

4. Divide icing into batches, and mix in different shades of food coloring to each. Transfer each to a pastry bag fitted with a small round tip (such as Ateco #2). Flood cookie with icing (see page 243).

5. Immediately pipe a red or blue dot in the center of cookie. Then pipe concentric rings of colors around the center dot (using the same color as the dot, or alternating colors).

6. Immediately drag a toothpick through the colors to create bursts, starting from the center dot and working toward the edge; then alternate dragging inward and outward as you work around the cookie. (Or drag around the cookie in one direction or curve the lines for a pinwheel effect.) Let dry. Repeat with remaining cookies and icings. (Decorated cookies can be stored in an airtight container at room temperature up to 3 days.)

Halloween Spiderweb Cookies

MAKES ABOUT 1 DOZEN

Your Halloween party guests will have fun working their way into the center of this alluring black-and-white web (just as the spider intended). Iced cookies are assembled in concentric circles, and then piped with black royal icing to form the web.

1 cup unbleached all-purpose flour

1 cup cake flour (not self-rising)

½ teaspoon baking powder

¼ teaspoon coarse salt

2 large eggs

¾ cup granulated sugar

½ cup whole milk

6 tablespoons unsalted butter, melted and cooled

½ teaspoon vanilla extract

2 cups confectioners' sugar, sifted

3 tablespoons hot water

2 tablespoons light corn syrup

Royal Icing (page 244)

Gel-paste food coloring in black

1. In a medium bowl, sift together both flours, baking powder, and salt. In a large bowl, whisk together eggs and granulated sugar until smooth. Add milk and whisk to combine. Whisk in melted butter and vanilla. Gradually add flour mixture and stir to form a smooth dough. Cover and chill for 1 hour.

2. Preheat oven to 350°F. Using a 2-ounce scoop, drop dough onto parchment-lined sheets, spacing 3 inches apart. Bake cookies, rotating sheets halfway through, until edges are light brown, 12 to 15 minutes. Transfer cookies to wire racks set over parchment and let cool completely.

3. In a small bowl, combine confectioners' sugar, hot water, and corn syrup. Whisk until smooth. Using a small offset spatula, spread icing on each cookie. Return cookies to rack to drip. Allow cookies to set, about 1 hour; transfer to a serving plate and arrange in tight concentric circles.

4. Meanwhile make royal icing (it should have the consistency of toothpaste; add more confectioners' sugar if needed). Tint royal icing with gel-paste food coloring until icing is black.

5. Transfer black royal icing to a pastry bag fitted with a small round tip (such as Ateco #2). Pipe a straight line from middle of top row of cookies to bottom. Pipe a second line going across middle of cookies, from left to right. Pipe 6 more lines through center point, spacing evenly apart; lines should form 16 even wedges. Create a web pattern by piping slightly curved, swooping lines to connect spokes, starting from center, letting icing flow between cookies; let set. (Cookies are best eaten the day they are made.)

Hamantaschen

MAKES 5 DOZEN

Served during the Jewish celebration of Purim, triangular preserves-filled hamantaschen symbolize the triumph of good over evil. The cookie's name means "Haman's pockets," but its shape also symbolizes the tricornered hat of the biblical story's villain. A poppy seed filling is the most traditional, but all sorts of jams work well with this buttery version of the dough.

2 sticks (1 cup) unsalted butter, room temperature

1½ cups granulated sugar

2 teaspoons finely grated orange zest plus 2 tablespoons fresh orange juice

2 teaspoons vanilla extract

3 large eggs, room temperature

4 cups unbleached all-purpose flour

4 teaspoons baking powder

½ teaspoon coarse salt

Store-bought jams, such as apricot, raspberry, and peach, for filling

Coarse sanding sugar, for sprinkling

1. In a large bowl, with an electric mixer on medium-high, beat butter and granulated sugar until pale and fluffy, about 3 minutes. Beat in orange zest and juice, vanilla, and 2 eggs until combined.

2. In another large bowl, whisk together flour, baking powder, and salt. Gradually add flour mixture to butter mixture and mix on low until just combined.

3. Divide dough into thirds. Place each third between 2 sheets of parchment. Roll dough to ⅛-inch thickness. Refrigerate until firm.

4. Using 3-inch round and 4-inch star cookie cutters, cut out shapes from dough. For triangles: Spoon ¾ teaspoon jam on each round; then shape by lifting sides of dough toward center, over filling, and pinching seams together. For stars: Spoon ½ teaspoon jam on each; lift points of dough to center, pinching seams at center.

5. Preheat oven to 350°F. Beat remaining egg in a small bowl. Brush cookies with egg wash; sprinkle with sanding sugar. Bake cookies, rotating sheets halfway through, until firm, 12 to 15 minutes. Transfer cookies to a wire rack and let cool completely. (Cookies can be stored in an airtight container at room temperature up to 5 days.)

TIPS

Some dos and don'ts will help these cookies retain their shape: Do chill the dough until it's firm, and don't overfill the cookies with jam (too much will cause them to spread out).

PERFECTING
ICED HEART COOKIES

Pink "paint" and edible gold dust launch these iced cookie hearts on an artful streak. Here we went for diagonal stripes, but with the variations on the following page you can work color both ways for a playful plaid, or dip cookies for a full-hearted (or colorful half-and-half) edible valentine. The dough is tender, so roll it between two sheets of floured parchment to keep it from sticking to the rolling pin. Dip the cutters in flour before each cut, and dust the spatula, too, before transferring the uncooked dough to the baking sheets.

MAKES ABOUT 2 DOZEN

2 cups unbleached all-purpose flour, plus more for dusting

½ teaspoon baking powder

½ teaspoon coarse salt

1 stick (½ cup) unsalted butter, room temperature

1 cup sugar

1 large egg, room temperature

1 teaspoon vanilla extract

Gel-paste food coloring (optional)

Royal Icing (page 244; optional)

Edible luster dust (optional)

Pure lemon extract (optional)

---

1. Make the cookies: In a medium bowl, whisk together flour, baking powder, and salt. In a large bowl, with an electric mixer on medium-high, beat butter and sugar until pale and fluffy, about 3 minutes. Beat in egg and vanilla. Reduce speed to low and gradually add flour mixture; beat until combined. Divide dough in half; form into disks, wrap each in plastic, and freeze until firm, about 20 minutes.

2. Preheat oven to 325°F. Remove one disk of dough; let stand 5 to 10 minutes. Roll out to ⅛-inch thickness between 2 sheets of lightly floured parchment, dusting with more flour as needed. Cut shapes with a 2½-inch heart-shaped cookie cutter. Using a spatula, transfer to parchment-lined baking sheets (if dough gets too soft, chill 10 minutes). Reroll scraps and cut more shapes. Repeat with remaining dough.

3. Bake cookies, rotating sheets halfway through, until edges are golden, about 12 minutes. Transfer to wire racks to cool completely.

continued

4. Decorate the cookies: If using, add gel-paste food coloring to royal icing, a drop at a time, until desired color is reached. Transfer royal icing to a bowl, hold a cookie face down, and gently dip it in, letting excess drip off and tapping gently to remove bubbles. Transfer iced cookies end to end to a wire rack, set over a baking sheet or piece of parchment, and let dry completely. Dilute gel food coloring with water, then, with a 2-inch-wide paintbrush, brush across them diagonally with pink "paint." In a small bowl, mix luster dust with a few drops of lemon extract. With a small brush, dot on gold specks. (Cookies can be stored in an airtight container at room temperature up to 1 week.)

ICED HEART VARIATIONS

Dipped

Bake heart cookies and allow to cool completely. Submerge half a heart in icing and scrape off the bottom on the bowl's edge. For gold specks, dot on edible luster dust mixed with a bit of lemon extract.

Plaid (not shown)

Pour icing into a bowl, hold a cookie face down, and gently dip it in, letting excess drip off and tapping gently to remove bubbles. Interlock iced cookies. Dilute gel-paste food coloring with water, then paint vertically and horizontally across the hearts with a 2-inch-wide brush, creating a plaid pattern.

Tips for Iced Heart Cookies

- This cookie should be very tender. Don't overmix the dough, as it will result in a tough cookie.

- Let the dough sit out of the freezer for 5 to 10 minutes before rolling out, so it's easier to work with. When rolling the dough, rotate it every few rolls to ensure an even thickness.

- Use an offset spatula when transferring the cookies to baking sheets so the shapes stay intact. If the dough is getting too soft, simply return it to the fridge for a few minutes.

- Before icing the cookies, place a parchment-lined baking sheet under the wire rack to catch any icing drips and for easier cleanup.

- For the painted brushstroke and plaid decorations, place the cookies close to one another on a baking sheet. This way you can brush over them all at once. Make sure to paint with very light strokes.

- If you want an icing with thinner consistency, which is usually used for flooding (see page 243), add more water. A thicker consistency is generally used for outlining and adding details.

8

THE BASICS

Learn the elements of cookie style—
drop, roll, slice, shape—and you'll be
well on your way to great baking.
Add icing, piping, and embellishing, and that's
where cookie perfection happens.

Techniques

Tips and tricks for mastering the foundations of cookie making, from shaping, slicing, and scooping to piping and decorating.

Slice-and-Bake Cookies

The dough for slice-and-bake cookies, fondly referred to as icebox cookies, can be made in advance and stored in the freezer.

Place dough on a sheet of parchment and shape into a rough log. Pull the parchment toward you over the log. To mold the dough, press the edge of a ruler along the two layers of parchment. Holding the bottom parchment, push the ruler tightly against the log to shape and smooth.

Cut open a paper-towel tube lengthwise and place the log inside (or roll log on a hard surface several times during the chilling process to prevent flattening). Refrigerate until firm, at least 3 hours. To bake, use a long, sharp knife to slice the frozen log.

Drop Cookies

Drop cookies are made by scooping spoonfuls of dough and "dropping" them on parchment-lined baking sheets.

The dough should be slightly firm. If it's too soft, refrigerate until firm, about 10 minutes. Use an ice-cream or cookie scoop (see page 18) to create uniform cookies, or use two tablespoons to shape them.

Space the cookies on the sheets, as they will spread in the oven. Cool them on the sheets for a few minutes, then transfer to a wire rack.

To make ahead, freeze unbaked balls of dough on sheets, then transfer to airtight containers and freeze up to 1 month. Bake frozen, adding a few minutes to the time.

Rolled and Cut

Perfectly rolled and cut cookies are the foundation for our showstopper cookies, like the Flower-Embellished Wreaths (page 24).

Divide the dough into equal disks and wrap in plastic. Chill in the refrigerator until firm, at least 1 hour, or according to recipe directions. To test if the dough is ready for rolling, press gently with your finger; it should barely leave an indentation.

Unwrap the dough and place it on a floured surface or between two sheets of parchment. (If the dough is sticky, lightly flour the parchment.) Beginning at the center

and applying even pressure, roll the dough between the parchment to the same thickness (to ensure the cookies bake at the same rate).

When cutting cookie shapes, begin at the outside of the dough and cut the shapes close together to minimize scraps. Refrigerate scraps until chilled, reroll, and cut again. In general, only reroll once, as the process toughens the dough.

Before baking, refrigerate the cut cookies on baking sheets until the dough is firm. Chilling will help maintain the shapes of the cut cookies as they bake.

Piping: Dough, Filling, and Icing

Piping gives you greater control when shaping the base of a heart (above left), or adding the perfect layer of creamy filling to a whoopie pie (above right), or flooding glossy icing on cutout cookies (opposite). While it may seem intimidating to a novice baker, it's surprisingly easy to master the basics. If it's your first time piping details, practice on parchment before getting started.

To fill a pastry bag, snip off the pointed end of a bag, then insert the coupler base into it, making sure the screw threads are covered. Place the pastry tip over the base of the coupler and screw on the outer ring to secure. Hold the bag with one hand and, to make filling it easy, fold down two to

three inches over your hand, or place the bag in a tall container or glass and fold the top over the sides. (Place a damp paper towel at the bottom to help keep the filling in the tip from drying out.) If the filling is runny, cover the tip with plastic wrap. Fill the bag halfway to two thirds, unfold the top, and push the filling toward the tip to get rid of any air bubbles. Twist the top of the bag to close or secure with a rubber band or binder clip.

Whether you're piping dough, filling, or icing, hold the top of the bag with one hand and direct the tip with the other. Keep the bag vertical, applying pressure as you go.

How to Pipe Royal Icing

1. With a ¼-inch round tip (such as Ateco #2), pipe an outline around the edge, leaving a ¼-inch border. Use a thick icing for the outline; then thin it with water, to a honey consistency, for Step 2.

2. Using a larger round tip (such as Ateco #5), pipe several zigzags across the entire surface to fill the outline. This is called flooding.

3. With a toothpick or a small offset spatula, spread the icing evenly over the cookie.

4. Allow the icing to dry about 12 hours before piping details. Once decorated, allow the cookies to dry completely, about 24 hours.

Icings, Fillings, and Glazes

Gorgeous piping, creamy fillings, and glossy glazes add beautiful color, contrasting textures, and sometimes that extra shine to enhance an already delicious treat.

Royal Icing

MAKES ABOUT 2 CUPS

1 pound (4 cups) confectioners' sugar, sifted, plus more if needed

¼ cup plus 1 tablespoon meringue powder

In a large bowl, with an electric mixer on low, beat confectioners' sugar, meringue powder, and scant ½ cup water until smooth and opaque white, about 7 minutes. If icing is too thick, add more water, 1 teaspoon at a time, beating until icing has the consistency of glue; if too thin, continue beating icing 2 to 3 minutes more, or add more sugar, 1 tablespoon at a time. Use immediately, or refrigerate in an airtight container up to 1 week; stir well with a flexible spatula before using.

VARIATION
To color the royal icing, add gel-paste food coloring, a drop or a dab at a time with a toothpick, and blend well before adding more, until desired color is reached.

Poured Chocolate Fondant

MAKES 1¾ CUPS

1½ pounds (6 cups) confectioners' sugar, sifted

2 tablespoons unsweetened Dutch-process cocoa powder

2 tablespoons light corn syrup

4 ounces unsweetened chocolate, finely chopped

In a medium saucepan, whisk together sugar and cocoa powder. Whisk in ½ cup water and the corn syrup; place over low heat and cook, stirring occasionally, until warm to the touch, about 4 minutes. Stir in chocolate until melted and smooth, about 1 minute more. Add additional warm water as needed to maintain a smooth consistency, and rewarm as needed in a microwave or in a bowl set over (not in) a pot of simmering water.

Basic Buttercream

MAKES 5½ CUPS

4 sticks (2 cups) unsalted butter, room temperature

1½ pounds (6 cups) confectioners' sugar, sifted

1 teaspoon vanilla extract

Pinch of coarse salt

In a large bowl, with an electric mixer on medium-high, beat butter until pale and creamy, about 2 minutes. With mixer on medium, add sugar, ½ cup at a time, beating after each addition, until combined, 1 to 2 minutes. Beat in vanilla and salt. Increase speed to medium-high and beat until smooth, about 1 minute more. Use immediately, or refrigerate in an airtight container up to 3 days. Before using, bring to room temperature and beat on low until smooth.

Caramel Buttercream

MAKES ABOUT 2 CUPS

⅓ cup sugar

Pinch of coarse salt

3 tablespoons heavy cream

2 teaspoons unsalted butter

1¼ cups Basic Buttercream (recipe at left)

1. In a small high-sided saucepan over medium heat, combine sugar, salt, and 2 tablespoons water, stirring until sugar is dissolved. Continue to cook, without stirring, washing down sides of pan with a wet pastry brush to prevent crystals from forming, until caramel is a deep amber, 8 to 10 minutes. Remove from heat.

2. Carefully whisk in cream (it will spatter), then butter, until combined. Let caramel sauce cool completely, about 45 minutes.

3. With mixer on medium, beat buttercream and caramel sauce, scraping down sides of bowl as necessary, until smooth, about 3 minutes. Use immediately or refrigerate in an airtight container up to 3 days. Before using, bring to room temperature and beat on low until smooth.

Swiss Meringue Filling

MAKES ABOUT 4 CUPS

4 large egg whites, room temperature

1 cup sugar

Pinch of cream of tartar

½ teaspoon vanilla extract

---

1. Fill a medium saucepan one-quarter full with water. Bring water to a simmer over medium heat.

2. In a heatproof bowl, combine egg whites, sugar, and cream of tartar; place over (not in) saucepan. Whisk constantly until sugar is dissolved and whites are warm to the touch, 3 to 3½ minutes. (Test by rubbing between your fingers.)

3. Remove bowl from heat. With an electric mixer on low, beat whites, gradually increasing to high speed, until stiff, glossy peaks form, about 10 minutes. Add vanilla and mix until just combined. (Use immediately, or refrigerate in an airtight container up to 3 days.)

Swiss Meringue Buttercream

MAKES ABOUT 6 CUPS

5 large egg whites, room temperature

1¼ cups sugar

4 sticks (2 cups) unsalted butter, cut into pieces, room temperature

1 teaspoon vanilla extract

1. Fill a medium saucepan one-quarter full with water. Bring water to a simmer over medium heat.

2. In a heatproof bowl, combine egg whites and sugar; place over (not in) saucepan. Whisk constantly until sugar is dissolved and whites are warm to the touch, 3 to 3½ minutes.

3. Remove bowl from heat. With an electric mixer on low, beat whites, gradually increasing to high speed, until stiff, glossy peaks form, about 10 minutes.

4. With mixer on low, add butter, piece by piece, to egg whites and beat until smooth. Add vanilla and mix until just combined. (Use immediately, or refrigerate in an airtight container up to 3 days.)

Lemon Glaze

MAKES ABOUT ¾ CUP

1 large egg white

2 cups confectioners' sugar, sifted, plus more if needed

1 to 2 teaspoons fresh lemon juice

In a large bowl, whisk together egg white, sugar, and 1 teaspoon lemon juice until smooth. If necessary, add up to 1 teaspoon lemon juice to reach desired consistency. If glaze runs down edges of cookie, add more sugar, 1 tablespoon at a time. If glaze is too thick, add water, 1 teaspoon at a time. (Use immediately, or store at room temperature, with plastic wrap pressed directly on surface, up to 2 days, or refrigerate up to 3 days. Bring to room temperature before using.)

Templates

To make the Honey-Spice Gingerbread Townhouses on page 205, photocopy these templates, enlarging them to 125%.

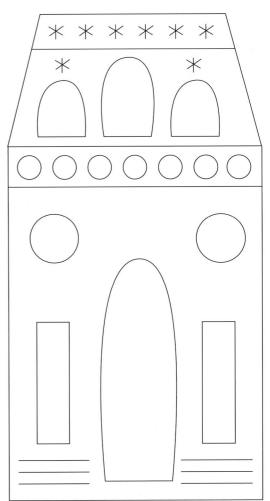

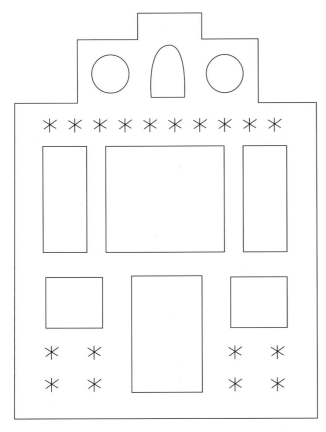

Embellishments

Making Sugared Garnishes

This technique can be used for mint leaves and small edible flowers, herb sprigs, and berries. In a small bowl, whisk together 1 egg white and 1 tablespoon water. Holding the mint leaf or other garnish with tweezers, brush egg white onto surface to lightly coat both sides. Sprinkle superfine sugar over surface and transfer to a wire rack set over a baking sheet to dry, about 8 hours. (Garnishes can be made 1 day ahead and kept in an airtight container at room temperature.)

Making Candied Citrus

With a sharp paring knife, slice the ends of oranges, lemons, or grapefruits. Following the curve of the fruit, cut away the outermost peel, leaving most of the white pith on the fruit. Slice the peel lengthwise into 1/4-inch-wide strips. In a medium pot of boiling water, cook peel until tender, about 10 minutes. With a slotted spoon, transfer peel to a wire rack set over a baking sheet; spread in a single layer to dry slightly, about 15 minutes. In a medium saucepan over high heat, bring 1 cup sugar and 1 cup water to a boil, stirring to dissolve sugar. Add peel and boil until it turns translucent and syrup thickens, 8 to 10 minutes. With slotted spoon, transfer peel to wire rack, separating the pieces as needed. Let peel dry 1 hour. Toss with 1/2 cup sugar to coat.

Making Candied Ginger

In a saucepan over medium heat, bring 2 cups sugar and 1 cup water to a boil. Cook, stirring, until sugar dissolves, about 5 minutes. Meanwhile, peel 2 pieces (6 inches each, about 8 ounces) fresh ginger. With a sharp paring knife, slice ginger crosswise very thinly (about 1/8 inch thick). Add ginger slices to pan; simmer over medium-low heat until translucent and tender, 20 to 25 minutes. With a slotted spoon, transfer ginger to a wire rack set over a baking sheet lined with parchment; let drain. Reserve ginger syrup for another use (let cool; refrigerate in an airtight container up to 1 month). Pour 1/4 cup sugar into a small bowl; coat ginger slices, 1 or 2 at a time, in sugar. (Store in an airtight container at room temperature up to 1 month.)

Toasting Nuts

To toast nuts such as almonds, pecans, and walnuts, preheat oven to 350°F. Spread nuts in a single layer on a rimmed baking sheet. Bake, tossing occasionally, until golden and fragrant, 10 to 12 minutes; start checking after 6 minutes if nuts are sliced or chopped. For hazelnuts, bake at 375°F until skins split, 10 to 12 minutes; when cool enough to handle, rub in a clean kitchen towel to remove skins.

Melting Chocolate

Coarsely chop chocolate with a serrated knife. Place chocolate in a dry heatproof bowl set over (not in) a pan of simmering water. Using a rubber spatula, gently stir chocolate until melted and shiny. Remove bowl from heat and wipe moisture from bottom of bowl.

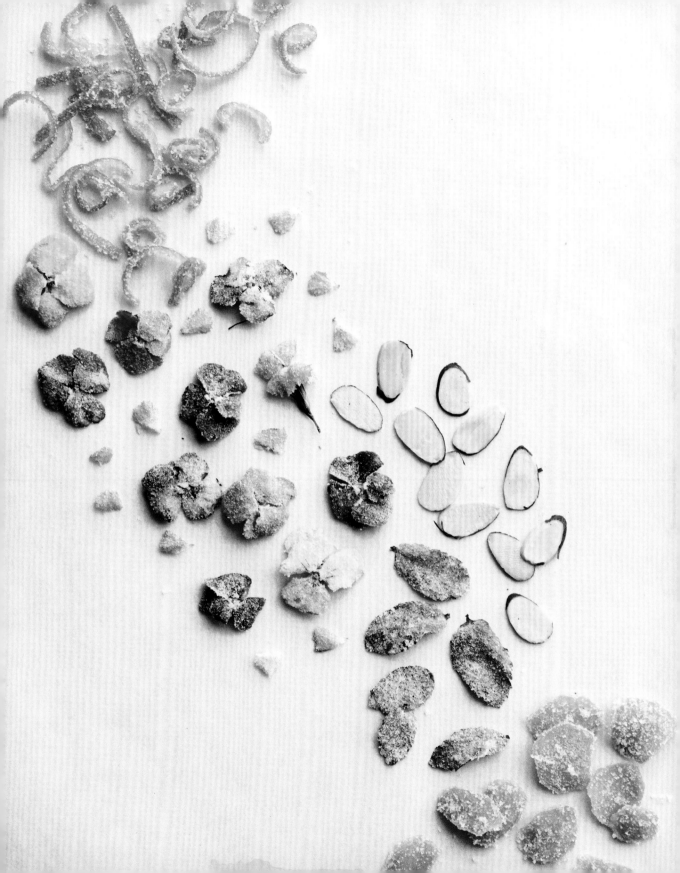

Thank You!

It has been more than ten years since our last book on cookies—a long time, considering how much we at Martha Stewart love baking, decorating, and eating them. Thank you to the editorial team of Susanne Ruppert, Sanaë Lemoine, and Nanette Maxim, who happily produced what we hope is your next favorite cookbook. Invaluable was Michael McCormick, who brilliantly created the beautiful design—from the colorful palette to the fresh, playful layouts. Food stylist Jason Schreiber skillfully took each cookie to the next level, and was ably assisted by the tireless Caitlin Haught Brown, Jess Damuck, and Molly Wenk. We were thrilled to be joined by photographer Lennart Weibull, who with the remarkable Lorie Reilly, effortlessly shot so many of the delicious-looking images. Prop stylist Carla Gonzalez-Hart helped ensure that the shots looked inviting. Thank you to the photographers listed below, whose work also graces these pages. Heartfelt thanks to Thomas Joseph, Kavita Thirupuvanam, and our colleagues and friends at *Living*, who were always ready to develop a new recipe, debate over baking techniques, or taste-test the latest batch of cookies. As always, special thanks to Kevin Sharkey and Carolyn D'Angelo. Other key players include Laura Wallis, Bridget Fitzgerald, Mike Varrassi, Stacey Tyrell, Gertrude Porter, and Josefa Palacios. We are pleased to be making books (and baking cookies) with our Clarkson Potter family, namely Jennifer Sit, Mark McCauslin, Linnea Knollmueller, Kim Tyner, Marysarah Quinn, Stephanie Huntwork, Jennifer Wang, Aaron Wehner, Doris Cooper, Kate Tyler, Stephanie Davis, and Jana Branson.

Photography Credits

All photographs by Lennart Weibull with the following exceptions:

Sidney Bensimon: Page 64
Anita Calero: Page 91
Chelsea Cavanaugh: Pages 29, 185, 234, 237
Ren Fuller: Page 99
Louise Hagger: Pages 37, 215, 220
Raymond Hom: Page 26
Mike Krautter: Pages 25, 41, 55, 56, 59, 103, 139, 154, 161, 162, 189, 193

Ryan Liebe: Page 76
David Malosh: Page 108
Johnny Miller: Page 228
Marcus Nilsson: Pages 52, 173
Linda Pugliese: Pages 110, 113
Armando Rafael: Cover, pages 67, 128
Jason Varney: Page 75
Anna Williams: Page 194
Linda Xiao: Page 51

Index